My Beautiful Lady by Thomas Woolner

Includes Nelly Dale

Thomas Woolner was born on 17th December 1825 in Hadleigh, Suffolk. He was primarily a sculptor and a part-time art dealer but also a founding member of the Pre-Raphaelite Brotherhood and, over time, a noted poet.

The poems here are excellent examples of Pre-Raphaelite poetry and brought praise from many including the very well thought of Victorian Poet Coventry Patmore. Parts of them were initially printed in the Pre-Raphaelites magazine 'The Germ' in 1850 before being expanded and published, as a whole, in 1863.

After helping to found the Pre-Raphaelite Brotherhood Woolner spent a year in Australia and returned to take up a career in Sculpture in earnest. Over the years, he was commissioned and created works of public importance including memorials, tombs and narrative reliefs.

As a man Woolner, was said to be a difficult character who had to make a concerted effort to rein in his personality and remain polite. However, he seemed to strike up a great number of friendships as well as offer advice. In the latter, he provided Tennyson with the scenario for his poem 'Enoch Arden'.

Between 1859 and 1864 Woolner was engaged to create a series of architectural sculptures for the Manchester Assize Courts. These statues depicted lawmakers and lawgivers and were part of the building's structure. Most dramatic was a giant sculpture depicting Moses which was placed above the entrance.

On 6th September 1864, he married Alice Gertrude Waugh, although initially he had proposed and been rejected by her sister, Fanny. The Woolners' had a large family of six children; four daughters and two sons.

Woolner gradually became disenchanted with much of what the Pre-Raphaelites stood for and later moved towards a more classical form of expression.

During the 1880s he returned to poetry to write three longer narrative works; Pygmalion, Silenus and Tiresias. These are much more in the classical vein in their exploration of eroticism.

On 7th October 1892, Thomas Woolner died, from a stroke, at the age of 66, in London.

Index of Contents

INTRODUCTION

"A ray has pierced me from the highest heaven—
I have believed in worth; and do believe."

So runs Mr. Woolner's song, as it proceeds to show the issue of a noble earthly love, one with the heavenly. Its issue is the life of high endeavour, wherein

"They who would be something more
Than they who feast, and laugh and die, will hear
The voice of Duty, as the note of war,
Nerving their spirits to great enterprise,
And knitting every sinew for the charge."

This Library is based on a belief in worth, and on a knowledge of the wide desire among men now to read books that are books, which "do," as Milton says, "contain a potency of life in them to be as active as that soul whose progeny they are; nay, they do preserve as in a vial the purest efficacy and extraction of that living intellect that bred them." When, therefore, as now happens for the second time, a man of genius who has written with a hope to lift the hearts and minds of men by adding one more true book to the treasures of the land, honours us by such recognition of our aim, and fellow-feeling with it, that he gives up a part of his exclusive right to his own work, and offers to make it freely current with the other volumes of our series,—we take the gift, if we may dare to say so, in the spirit of the giver, and are the happier for such evidence that we are not working in vain.

Such evidence comes in other forms: as in letters from remote readers in lonely settlements, from the far West, from sheep-farms in Australia, from farthest India, from places to which these little volumes make their way as pioneers; being almost the first real books that have there been seen. To send a true voice over, for delight and support of earnest workers who open their hearts wide to a good book in a way that we can hardly understand,—we who live wastefully in the midst of plenty, and are apt sometimes to leave to feed on the fair mountain and batten on the moor,—is worth the while of any man of genius who puts his soul into his work, as Mr. Woolner does.

Books in the "National Library" that come like those of Mr. Patmore and Mr. Woolner are here as friends and companions. If they were not esteemed highly they would not be here. Beyond that implied opinion there is nothing to be said. He would be an ill-bred host who criticized his guest, or spoke loud praise of him before his face. Nor does a well-known man of our own day need personal introduction. It is only said, in consideration that this book will be read by many who cannot know what is known to those who have access to the works of artists, that Mr. Thomas Woolner is a Royal Academician, and one of the foremost sculptors of our day. For a couple of years, from 1877 to 1879, he was Professor of Sculpture at the Royal Academy. A colossal statue by him in bronze of Captain Cook was designed for a site overlooking Sydney Harbour. A poet's mind has given life to his work on the marble, and when he was an associate with Mr. Millais, Mr. Holman Hunt, and others, who, in 1850, were endeavouring to bring truth and beauty of expression into art, by the bold reaction against tame and insincere conventions for which Mr. Ruskin pleaded and which the time required, Mr. Woolner joined in the production by them of a magazine called "The Germ," to which some of the verses in this volume were contributed.

There is no more to say; but through another page let Wordsworth speak the praise of Books:

     Yet is it just
That here, in memory of all books which lay
Their sure foundations in the heart of man,
Whether by native prose, or numerous verse.
That in the name of all inspired souls—
From Homer the great thunderer, from the voice
That roars along the bed of Jewish song,
And that more varied and elaborate,
Those trumpet tones of harmony that shake
Our shores in England—from those loftiest notes,
Down to the low and wren-like warblings, made
For cottagers and spinners at the wheel
And sunburnt travellers resting their tired limbs
Stretched under wayside hedgerows, ballad tunes
Food for the hungry ears of little ones
And of old men who have survived their joys—
'Tis just that in behalf of these, the works,
And of the men that framed them, whether known
Or sleeping nameless in their scattered graves,
That I should here assert their rights, attest
Their honours, and should, once for all, pronounce
Their benediction; speak of them as Powers
For ever to be hallowed; only less,
For what we are and what we may become,
Than Nature's self, which is the breath of God,
Or His pure Word by miracle revealed.

Prelude, Book V.

Henry Morley

MY BEAUTIFUL LADY

THE INTRODUCTION

In some there lies a sorrow too profound
To find a voice or to reveal itself
Throughout the strain of daily toil, or thought,
Or during converse born of souls allied,
As aught men understand. And though mayhap
Their cheeks will thin or droop; and wane their eyes'
Frank lustre; hair may lose its hue, or fall;
And health may slacken low in force; and they
Are older than the warrant of their years;
Yet they to others seem to gild their lives
With cheerfulness, and every duty tend,
As if their aspects told the truth within.

But they are not as others: not for them
The bounding pulse, and ardour of desire,
The rapture and the wonder in things new;
The hope that palpitating enters where
Perfection smiles on universal life;
Nor do they with elastic enterprise
Forecast delight in compassing results;
Nor, having won their ends, fall godlike back
And taste the calm completion of content.
But in a sober chilled grey atmosphere
Work out their lives; more various though they are
Than creatures in the unknown ocean depths,
Yet each in whom this vital grief has root
Is dull to what makes everything of worth.
And though, may be, a shallow bodily joy
Oft tingles through them at the breathing spring,
Or first-heard exultation of the lark;
Still that deep weight draws ever steadily
Their thoughts and passions back to secret woe.
Though, if endowed with light, heroic deeds
May be achieved; and if benignly bent
They may be treasured blessings through their lives;
Yet power and goodness are to them as dreams,
And they heed vaguely, if their waking sight

Be met with slanting storm against the pane,
Or sunshine glittering on the leaves that play
In purest blue of breezy summer morns.

Whence springs this well of mournfulness profound,
Unfathomable to plummet cast by man?
Alas; for who can tell! Whence comes the wind
Heaving the ocean into maddened arms
That clutch and dash huge vessels on the rocks,
And scatter them, as if compacted slight
As little eggs boys star against a tree
In wanton mischief? Whence, detestable,
To man, who suffers from the monster-jaws,
The power that in the logging crocodiles'
Outrageous bulk puts evil fire of life?
That spouts from mountain-pyramids a flood
Of lava, overwhelming works and men
In burning, fetid ruin?—The power that stings
A city with a pestilence: or turns
The pretty babe, who in his mother's lap
Babbles her back the lavished kiss and laugh,
Through lusts and vassalage to obdurate sin,
Into a knife-armed midnight murderer?

Our lives are mysteries, and rarely scanned
As we read stories writ by mortal pen.
We can perchance but catch a straying weft
And trace the hinted texture here or there,
Of that stupendous loom weaving our fates.
Two parents, late in life, are haply blessed
With one bright child, a wonder in his years,
For loveliness and genius versatile:
Some common ill destroys him; parents, both,
Until their death, are left but living tombs
That hold the one dead image of their joy.
A man, the flower of honour, who has found
His well-beloved young daughter fled from home,
Fallen from her maidenhood, a nameless thing
Tainting his blood. A youth who throws the strength
Of his whole being into love for one
Answering him honeyed smiles, and leaves his land
For some far country, seeking wealth he hopes
Will grace her daintily with choice delights,
And on returning sees the honeyed smiles
Are sweetening other lips. A husband who
Has found that household curse, a faithless wife.
A thinker whose far-piercing care perceives
His nation goes the road that ends in shame.

A gracious woman whose reserve denies
The power to utter what consumes her heart.
Such instances (and some a loss to know,
Which steadfast reticence will shield from those,
Debased or garrulous, whose hearts corrupt,
But learn the gloomy secrets of their kind
To poison-tip their wit, or grope and grin
With pharisaic laughter at disgrace)—
Such instances as these demand no guide
To thrid the dismal issues from their source!
But others are there, lying fast concealed,
Dark, hopeless, and unutterably sad,
Which have not been, and never may be known.

Then we may well call happy one whose grief,
Mixed up with sacred memories of the past,
Can tell to others how the tempest rose,
That struck and left him lonely in the world;
And who, narrating, feels his sorrow soothed,
By that respect which love and sorrow claim.

It much behoves us all, but chiefly those
Whom fate has favoured with an easy trust,
To keep a bridle upon restless speech
And thought: and not in flagrant haste prejudge
The first presentment as the rounded truth.
For true it is, that rapid thoughts, and freak
Of skimming word, and glance, more frequently
Than either malice, settled hate, or scorn,
Support confusion, and pervert the right;
Set up the weakling in the strong man's place;
And yoke the great one's strength to idleness;
Pour gold into the squanderer's purse, and suck
The wealth, which is a power, from their control
Who would have turned it unto noble use.
And oftentimes a man will strike his friend,
By random verbiage, with sharper pain
Than could a foe, yet scarcely mean him wrong;
For none can strip this complex masquerade
And know who languishes with secret wounds.
They whom the brunt of war has maimed in limb,
Who lean on crutches to sustain their weight,
Are manifest to all; and reverence
For their misfortunes kindly gains them place:
But wounds, sometimes more deep and dangerous,
We may in careless jostle through the crowd,
Gall and oppress, because to us unknown.
Then, howsoever by our needs impelled,

Let us resolve to move in gentleness;
Judge mildly when we doubt; and pause awhile
Before injustice palpably proclaimed
Ere we let fall the judgment stroke: against
Their ignominious craft, who ever wait
To filch another's right, we will maintain
Majestic peace in silence; knowing well
Their craft takes something richer from themselves.
It is but seemly to respect the great;
But never let us fail toward lowly ones;
Respecting more, in that they lack the force
To claim it of the world. For souls there are
Of poor capacities, whose purpose holds,
Throughout their unregarded lives, a worth,
And earnest law of fixed integrity,
That were an honour even unto those
Whose genius marks the boundaries of our race.

PART THE FIRST

LOVE

Love comes divinely, gladdening mortal life,
As sunrise dawns upon the gaze of one
Bewildered in some outland waste, and lost:
Who, lonely faint and shuddering, through the night
Heard savage creatures nigh; and far-off moan
Of tempests on the wind.

    Auroral joy
Flushes the brow of childhood, warms his cheek
To rosier redness at the name of Love;
And earlier thoughts awake in darkness strive;
As unfledged nestlings move their sightless heads
At sound, toward a fair world to them unknown.
Young Hope scales azure mountain heights to gaze,
In Love's first golden and delicious dream.
He sees the earth a maze of tempting paths,
For blissful sauntering mid the crowded flowers
And music of the rills. No ambushed wrongs,
Or thwarting storms there baffle and surprise;
But lingering, man treads long an odorous way;
And at the close, with Love clasped hand in hand,
Sets in proud glory: thence to rise anon
With Love beyond the stars and rest in heaven.

Man, nerved by Love, can steadily endure
Clash of opposing interests; perplexed web
Of crosses that distracting clog advance:
In thickest storm of contest waxes stronger
At momentary thought of home, of her,
His gracious wife, and bright-faced joys.

    To him
The wrinkled patriarch, who,sits and suns
His shrunken form beneath the boughs he climbed
A lissom boy, whence comes that brooding smile,
Whose secret lifts his cheeks, and overflows
His sight with tender dew? What through his frame
Melts languor sweeter than approaching sleep
To one made weary by a hard day's toil?
It is the memory of primal love,
Whose visionary splendour steeped his life
In hues of heaven; and which grown open day,
Revealing perilous falls, his steps confined
Within the pathways to the noblest end.
Now following this dimmed glory, tired, his soul
Haunts ever the mysterious gates of Death;
And waits in patient reverence till his doom
Unfolding them fulfils immortal Love.

As from some height, on a wild day of cloud,
A wanderer, chilled and worn, perchance beholds
Move toward him through the landscape soaked in gloom
A golden beam of light; creating lakes,
And verdant pasture, farms, and villages;
And touching spires atop to flickering flame;
Disclosing herds of sober feeding kine;
And brightening on its way the woods to song;
As he, that wanderer, brightens when the shaft
Suddenly falls on him. A moment warmed,
He scarcely feels its loveliness before
The light departing leaves his saddened soul
More cold than ere it came.
    Thus love once shone
And blessed my life: so vanished into gloom.

I. MY BEAUTIFUL LADY

I love My Lady; she is very fair;
Her brow is wan, and bound by simple hair:
   Her spirit sits aloof, and high,
   But glances from her tender eye

In sweetness droopingly.

As a young forest while the wind drives through,
My life is stirred when she breaks on my view;
  Her beauty grants my will no choice
  But silent awe, till she rejoice
    My longing with her voice.

Her warbling voice, though ever low and mild,
Oft makes me feel as strong wine would a child:
  And though her hand be airy light
  Of touch, it moves me with its might,
    As would a sudden fright.

A hawk high poised in air, whose nerved wing-tips
Tremble with might suppressed, before he dips,
  In vigilance, hangs less intense
  Than I, when her voice holds my sense
    Contented in suspense.

Her mention of a thing, august or poor,
Makes it far nobler than it was before:
  As where the sun strikes life will gush,
  And what is pale receive a flush,
    Rich hues, a richer blush.

My Lady's name, when I hear strangers use,
Not meaning her, sounds to me lax misuse;
  I love none but My Lady's name;
  Maud, Grace, Rose, Marian, all the same,
    Are harsh, or blank and tame.

My Lady walks as I have seen a swan
Swim where a glory on the water shone:
  There ends of willow branches ride,
  Quivering in the flowing tide,
    By the deep river's side.

Fresh beauties, howsoe'er she moves, are stirred:
As the sunned bosom of a humming bird
  At each pant lifts some fiery hue,
  Fierce gold, bewildering green or blue;
    The same, yet ever new.

What time she walks beneath the flowering May,
Quite sure am I the scented blossoms say,
  "O Lady with the sunlit hair!
  Stay and drink our odorous air,

The incense that we bear:

"Thy beauty, Lady, we would ever shade;
For near to thee, our sweetness might not fade."
  And could the trees be broken-hearted,
  The green sap surely must have smarted,
    When my Lady parted.

How beautiful she is! A glorious gem
She shines above the summer diadem
  Of flowers! And when her light is seen
  Among them, all in reverence lean
    To her, their tending Queen.

A man so poor that want assaults his health,
Blessed with relief one morn in boundless wealth,
  Breathes no such joy as mine, when she
  Stands statelier, expecting me,
    Than tall white lilies be:

And the white flutter of her robe to trace,
Where clematis and jasmine interlace,
  Expands my gaze triumphantly:
  Even such his gaze, who sees on high
    His flag, for victory.

We wander forth unconsciously, because
The azure beauty of the evening draws;
  When sober hues pervade the ground,
  And universal life is drowned
    Into hushed depths of sound.

We thread a copse where frequent bramble spray
With loose obtrusion from the side roots stray,
  And force sweet pauses on our walk;
  I lift one with my foot, and talk
    About its leaves and stalk.

Or maybe that some thorn or prickly stem
Will take a prisoner her long garments' hem;
  To disentangle it I kneel,
  Oft wounding more than I can heal;
    It makes her laugh, my zeal.

Or on before a thin-legged robin hops,
And leaping on a twig, he pertly stops,
  Speaking a few clear notes, till nigh
  We draw, when briskly he will fly

Into a bush close by.

A flock of goldfinches arrest their flight,
And wheeling round a birchen tree alight
　Deep in its glittering leaves; and stay
　Till scared at our approach, when they
　　Strike with vexed trills away.

I recollect My Lady in the wood,
Keeping her breath, while peering as she stood
　There, balanced lightly on tiptoe,
　To mark a nest built snug below,
　　Leaves shadowing her brow.

I recollect her puzzled, asking me,
What that strange tapping in the wood might be?
　I told of gourmand thrushes, which,
　To feast on morsels oosy rich,
　　Cracked poor snails' curling niche.

And then, as knight led captive, in romance,
Through postern and dark passage, past grim glance
　Of arms; where from throned state the dame
　He loved, in sumptuous blushes came
　　To him held dumb for shame:

Even so my spirit passed, and won, through fears
That trembled nigh despair; through foolish tears,
　And hope fallen weak in breathless flight,
　Where beamed in pure entrancing light
　　Love's beauty on my sight.

For when we reached a hollow, where the stone
And scattered fragments of the shells lay strown,
　By margin of a weedy rill;
　"This air," she said, "feels damp and chill,
　　We'll go home if you will."

"Make not my pathway dull so soon," I cried;
"See how yon clouds of rosy eventide
　Roll out their splendour: while the breeze
　Shifts gold from leaf to leaf, as these
　　Lithe saplings move at ease!"

Grateful, in her deep silence, one loud thrush
Startled the air with song; then every bush
　Of covert songsters all awoke,
　And all, as to their leader's stroke,

Into full chorus broke.

A lonely wind sighed up the pines, and sung
Of woes long past, forgot. My spirit hung
  O'er awful gulfs: and loathly dread
  So bitter was I wished me dead,
    And from a great void said;

"Wait till its glory fade; the sun but burned
To light your loveliness!" The Lady turned
  To me, flushed by its lingering rays,
  Mute as a star. My frantic praise
    Fixed wide her brightened gaze:

When, rapt in resolution, I told all
The mighty love I bore her; how would pall
  My very breath of life, if she
  For ever breathed not hers with me:—
    Could I a spirit be,

How, vainly hoping to enrich her grace,
What gems and wonders would I snatch from space;
  Would back through the vague distance beat,
  Glowing with joy her smile to meet,
    And heap them round her feet!

Her waist shook to my arm. She bowed her head
To mine in silence, and my fears had fled:
  (Just then we heard a tolling bell.)
  Ah no; it is not right to tell;
    But I remember well

How dear the pressure of her warm young breast
Against my own, her home; how proud and blessed
  I stood and felt her trickling tears,
  While proudly murmuring in her ears
    The hope of distant years.

The rest I keep: a holy charm, a source
Of secret strength and comfort on my course.
  Her glory left my pathway bright;
  And stars on stars throughout the night
    Came blooming into light.

II. DAWN

O lily with the heavenly sun
  Shining upon thy breast!
My scattered passions toward thee run,
  And poise to awful rest.

The darkness of our universe
  Smothered my soul in night;
Thy glory shone; whereat the curse
  Passed molten into light.

Raised over envy; freed from pain;
  Beyond the storms of chance:
Blessed king of my own world I reign,
  Controlling circumstance.

III. NOON

Warble, warble, warble, O thou joyful bird!
Warble, lost in leaves that shade my happy head;
Warble loud delights, laud thy warm-breasted mate,
And warbling shout the riot of thy heart,
Thine utmost rapture cannot equal mine.

Flutter, flutter, and flash; crimson-winged flower,
Parted from thy stem grown in land of dreams!
Hover and tremble, flitting till thou findest,
Butterfly, thy treasure! Yet thou never canst
Find treasure rich as my contented rest.

Hum on contentedly, thou wandering bee!
Or pausing in chosen flowers drain their sweets;
From honeyed petal thou canst never sip
The sweetest sweet of sweets, as I from Love,—
From Love's warm mouth draw sweetest sweet of sweets.

Round, western wind, in grateful eddies sway,
Whisper deliciously the trembling flowers:
O could I fill thy vacancy as I
Am filled with happiness, thou'dst breathe such sounds
Their blooms should wane and waver sick for love;
Thou'dst utter rarer secrets than are blown
With yonder bean-fields' paradisal scents;—
These bean-field odours, lightly sweet and faint,
That tell of pastures sloping down to streams
Murmuring for ever on through sunny lands;
Where mountains gleam and bank to silvery heights
That scarce the greatest angel's wing can reach;

Where wondrous creatures float beneath the shade
Of growths sublime, unknown to mortal race;
Where hazes opaline lie tranced in dreams,
Where melodies are heard and die at will,
And little spirits make hot love to flowers.

Though broadly flaming, plain of yellow blossom,
A dazzling blaze of splendour in the noon!
And brightening open heaven, ye shining clouds,
With lustrous light that casts the azure dim!
Your radiance all united to the sun's
Were darkness to that glory born in me.

For Love's own voice has owned her love is mine;
And Love's own palm has pressed my palm to hers;
Love's own deep eyes have looked the love she spoke:
And Love's young heart to mine was fondly beating
As from her lips I sucked the sweet of life.

IV. NIGHT

What trite old folly unharmonious sages
In dull books write or prattle day by day,
Of sin original and growing crime!
And commentating the advance of time,
Say wrong has fostered wrong for countless ages,
The strong ones marking down the weak for prey.

They bruit of wars—that thunder heard in dreams;
Huge insurrections, and dynastic changes
Resolved in blood. I marvel they of thought
By apprehensions are so often wrought
To state as fact what unto all men seems,
Who watch cloud-struggles blown through stormy ranges!

Why fill they not with love the printed page,
Illuminating, as yon moon the night,
Serenely shining on a world of beauty,
Where love moves ever hand in hand with duty;
And life, a long aspiring pilgrimage,
Makes labour but a pastime of delight!

It was delightfulness to him I found
Whistling this afternoon behind his team,
That stepped an easy comfortable pace;
While off the mould-iron curved in rolling grace

Dark earth, wave lapping wave, without a sound;
And all passed by me blissful, like a dream.

And those I noticed hoeing on the hill
Talking familiarly of homely things,
A daughter's marriage-day, a son's first child;
How the good Squire at length was reconciled,
Had overlooked the pheasant shot by Will:—
Chirruping on as any cricket sings.

And that complete Arcadian pastoral,
The piping boy who watched his feeding sheep;
And, as a little bird o'erflows with joy,
Piped on for hours my happy shepherd boy!
While, coiled below, his faithful animal
Basked in the sunshine, blinking, half asleep.

This silent night-wind bloweth heavenly pure;
Like dimpled warmth of an infantine face.
Lo, glimmering starlike in yon balmy vale
The village lights; each tells a little tale
Of humble comfort, where its inmates, sure
In hope, feel grateful in their lowly place.

And here My Lady's lighted oriel shines
A giant glowworm in the odorous gloom.
Ah, stands she smiling there in loose white gown,
Hearing the music of her future drown
The stillness and hushed whispering of the vines,
Whose lattice-clasping leaves o'ershade her room!

Or kneels she worshipful beside her bed
In large-eyed hope and bended lowliness,
To crave that He, the Giver, may impart
Enough of strength to bind her trembling heart
Steadfast and true; and that her will be led
To own His chastening cares pain but to bless?

Or sits she at her mirror, face to face
With her own loveliness? (O blessed land
That owns such twin perfections both together;
If guessed aright!) Ah, me; I wonder whether
She now her braided opulent hair unlace
And drop it billowing from her moonwhite hand!

Then what a fount of wealth to lover's sight!
Her loosened hair, I heard her mother say,
When she is seated, tumbles to the floor

And trails the length of her own foot and more:
And dare I, lapt in bliss, dream my delight
Ere long shall watch its rippling softness play?

Dare I, O vanity! but do I dare
Think she now looks upon the sorry rhyme
I wrote long ere that well-loved setting sun,
What time love conquering dread My Lady won,
While I unblessed, adored in mute despair:—
Even now I gave it her at parting time.

"O let me, Dearest, fall and once impart
My grieving love to ease this stricken heart;
    But once, O Love, to fall and rest
        This wearied head of mine,
        But once to weep in thine
    Unutterably tender breast;
And on my drooping lids feel thy young breath;
To feel it playing sweeter were than death.

"Than death were sweet to one bent down and old,
And worn with persecutions manifold;
    Whose stoutness long endured alone
        The charge of bitter foes,
        Till, furious, he rose,
    When smitten, all were overthrown.
Who then of those, his dearest, none could find,
They having fled as leaves before the wind.

"As he would pass, when to his failing sight
Their forms stand in a vision heavenly bright;
    And piercing through his drowsed ears
        Enters their tuneful cry
        Of summons, audibly,
    Thither where flow no mourners' tears:
So, dearest Love, my spirit, sore oppressed,
Would weeping in thy bosom sink to rest."

Her window now is darkness, save the sheen
Glazed on it by the moon. Within she lies
Her supple shape relaxed, in dreamful rest,
And folds contentment babelike to her breast,
Whose beauteous heaving, even and serene,
Beats mortal time to heavenly lullabies.

V. WILD ROSE

To call My Lady where she stood
"A Wild-rose blossom of the wood,"
Makes but a poor similitude.

For who by such a sleight would reach
An aim, consumes the worth in speech,
And sets a crimson rose to bleach.

My Love, whose store of household sense
Gives duty golden recompense,
And arms her goodness with defence:

The sweet reliance of whose gaze
Originates in gracious ways,
And wins the trust that trust repays:

Whose stately figure's varying grace
Is never seen unless her face
Turn beaming toward another place;

For such a halo round it glows
Surprised attention only knows
A lively wonder in repose.

Can flowers that breathe one little day
In odorous sweetness life away,
And wavering to the earth decay,

Have any claim to rank with her,
Warmed in whose soul impulses stir,
Then bloom to goodness, and aver

Her worth through spheral joys shall move
When suns and systems cease above,
And nothing lives but perfect Love?

VI. MY LADY'S GLORY

Strong in the regal strength of love,
  Enthroned by native worth
  Her sway is held on earth:
Whose soul looks downward from above
  Exalted stars, whose power
  Brightens the brightest flower.

Her beauty walks in happier grace
  Than lightly moving fawns
  O'er old elm-shadowed lawns.
A tenderness shows through her face,
  And like the morning's glow,
  Hints a full day below.

When site looks wide around the skies
  On the sun's dazzling track,
  And when shines softly back
Its glory to her open eyes,
  She fills our hearts and sight
  With wonder and delight.

And when tired thought my sense benumbs,
  Or when past shadows roll
  Their memories on my soul,
Oft breaking through the darkness comes
  A solace and surprise,
  Her wonder-lighted eyes.

How grand and beautiful the love
  She silently conceals,
  Nor save in act reveals!
She broods o'er kindness; as a dove
  Sits musing in the nest
  Of the life beneath her breast.

The ready freshness that was known
  In man's authentic prime,
  The earliest breath of time,
Throughout her household ways is shown;
  Mild greatness subtly wrought
  With quaint and childlike thought.

She sits to music: fingers fall,
  Air shakes; her lifted voice
  Makes flattered hope rejoice,
And shivering through Time's phantom pall,
  Its wavering rents display
  Dim splendour, far away;

Where her perfection, glory-crowned,
  Shall rest in love for ever;
  When mortal systems sever,
And the orbed universe is drowned,
  Leaving the empty skies
  The blank of death-closed eyes.

Deep in this truth I root my trust;
  And know the dear One's praise,
  Her mutely gracious ways,
When all her loveliness is dust
  And mosses rase her name,
  Will bless our world the same.

As scent of flowers her worth was born
  Her joyous goodness spread
  Like music over head,
Smiles now as smiles a plain of corn
  When in the winds of June,
  Lit by a shining noon.

A gap of sunlight in the storm;
  A blossom ere the spring;
  Immortal whispering;
A spirit manifest through form
  Which we can touch and kiss,—
  To life such beauty is.

Ah! who can doubt, though he may doubt
  Our solid earth will run
  A future round the sun,
That gentle impulse given out
  Can never fail or die,
  But throbs eternally!

VII. HER SHADOW

At matin time where creepers interlace
We sauntered slowly, for we loved the place,
And talked of passing things; I, pleased to trace
Through leafy mimicry the true leaves made,
The stateliness and beauty of her shade;

A wavering of strange purples dimly seen,
It gloomed the daisy's light, the kingcup's sheen,
And drank up sunshine from the vital green.
That silent shadow moving on the grass
Struck me with terror it should ever pass

And be blank nothing in the coming years
Where, in the dreadful shadow of my fears,
Her shrouded form I saw through blurring tears,

My Darling's shrouded form in beauty's bloom
Born with funereal sadness to her tomb.

"What idle dreaming," I abruptly cried:
My Lady turned, half startled, at my side,
And looked inquiry: I, through shame or pride,
Bantered the words as mockery of sense,
Mere aimless freak of fostered indolence.

She did not urge me; gentle, wise, and kind!
But clasped my hand and talked: her beaming mind
Arrayed in brightness all it touched. Behind,
Her shadow fell forgot, as she and I
Went homeward musing, smiling at the sky.

Thro' pastures and thro' fields where corn grew strong;
By cottage nests that could not harbour wrong;
Across the bridge where laughed the stream; along
The road to where her gabled mansion stood,
Old, tall, and spacious, in a massy wood.

We loitered toward the porch; but paused meanwhile
Where Psyche holds a dial to beguile
The hours of sunshine by her golden smile;
And holds it like a goblet brimmed with wine,
Nigh clad in trails of tangled eglantine.

In the deep peacefulness which shone around
My soul was soothed: no darksome vision frowned
Before my sight while cast upon the ground
Where Psyche's and My Lady's shadows lay,
Twin graces on the flower-edged gravel way.

I then but yearned for Titian's glorious power,
That I by toiling one devoted hour,
Might check the march of Time, and leave a dower
Of rich delight that beauty I could see,
For broadening generations yet to be.

VIII. HER GARDEN

The wind that's good for neither man nor beast
Weeks long incessant from the blighting East
Drove gloom and havoc through the land and ceased.
When swaying mildly over wide Atlantic seas,
Bland and dewy soft streamed the Western breeze.

In walking forth, I felt with vague alarm,
Closer than wont her pressure on my arm,
As through morn's fragrant air we sought what harm
That Eastern wind's despite had done the garden growth;
Where much lay dead or languished low for drouth.

Her own parterre was bounded by a red
Old buttressed wall of brick, moss-broidered;
Where grew mid pink and azure plots a bed
Of shining lilies intermixed in wondrous light;
She called them "Radiant spirits robed in white."

Here the mad gale had rioted and thrown
Far drifts of snowy petals, fiercely blown
The stalks in twisted heaps: one flower alone
Yet hung and lit the waste, the latest blossom born
Among its fallen kinsmen left forlorn.

"Thy pallid droop," cried I, "but more than all,
Thy lonely sweetness takes my soul in thrall,
O Seraph Lily Blanch! so stately tall:
By violets adored, regarded by the rose,
Well loved by every gentle flower that blows!"

My Lady dovelike to the lily went,
Took in curved palms a cup, and forward leant,
Deep draining to the gold its dreamy scent.
I see her now, pale beauty, as she bending stands,
The wind-worn blossom resting in her hands!

Then slowly rising, she in gazing trance
Affrayed, long pored on vacancy. A glance
Of chilly splendour tinged her countenance
And told the saddened truth, that stress of blighting weather,
Had made her lilies and My Lady droop together.

IX. TOLLING BELL

"Weak, but her spirits good," the letter said:
A bell was tolling, while these words I read,
A dull sepulchral summons for the dead.
　　Fear grew in every pace I strode
　　Hurrying on that endless road.

And when I reached the house a terror came

That wrought in me a hidden sense of blame,
And entering I scarce dared to speak her name,
  Who lay, sweet singer, warbling low
  Rhymes I made her long ago.

  "The sun exhales the morning dew,
    The dew returns again
    At eve refreshing rain:
  The forest flowers bloom bravely new,
    They drooping fade and die,
    The seeds that in them lie
  Will blossom as the others blew."

  "And ever rove among the flowers
    Bright children who ere long
    Are men and women strong:
  When on they pass through sun and showers,
    And glancing sideways watch
    Their children run to catch
  A rainbow with the laughing Hours."

I watched in awkward wonder for a time
As there she listless lay and sang my rhyme,
Wrapped up in fabrics of an Indian clime
  She seemed a Bird of Paradise
  Languid from the traversed skies.

A dawn-bright snowy peak her smile . . . Strange I
Should dawdle near her grace admiringly,
When love alarmed and challenged sympathy,
  Announced in chills of creeping fear
  Danger surely threatening near.

I shrank from searching the abyss I felt
Yawned by; whose verge voluptuous blossoms belt
With dazzling hues:—she speaks! I fall and melt,
  One sacred moment drawn to rest,
  Deeply weeping in her breast:

Within the throbbing treasure wept? But brief
Those loosening tears of blessed deep relief,
That won triumphant ransom from my grief,
  While loving words and comfort she
  Breathed in angel tones to me.

Our visions met, when pityingly she flung
Her passionate arms about me, kissing clung,
Close kisses, stifling kisses; till each wrung,

With welded mouths, the other's bliss
Out in one long sighing kiss.

Love-flower that burst in kisses and sweet tears,
Scattering its roseate dreamflakes, disappears
Into cold truth: for, loud with brazen jeers,
  That bell's toll, clanging in my brain,
  Beat me, loth, to earth again:

Where, looking on my Love's endangered state,
Wrought by keen anguish mad, I struck at fate,
Prostrating mockingly in sport or hate
  The aspirations, darkling, we
  Cherish and resolve to be.

She spoke, but sharply checked; then as her zone
A lady's hands would clasp, My Lady's own
Pressed at her yielding side; her solemn tone
  And forward eager face implored
  Me to kneel where she adored.

Despite her pain, with tender woman's phrase
She solaced me, whose part it was to raise
Anew the gladness to her weakened gaze,
  And wisely in man's firmness be
  To my drooping vine a tree.

But no; sunk, dwindled, dwarfed, and mean, beside
Her couch I sitting saw her eyes grow wide
With awe, and heard her voice move as the tide
  Of steady music rich and calm
  In some high cathedral psalm.

Then, as that high cathedral psalm o'erflows
The dusky, vaulted aisles, and slowly grows
A burst of harmony the hearer knows,
  Her voice assailed by rage, and I
  Took its purport wonderingly.

"Ah, pause for dread, before you charge in haste
The ways of fate; for how can those be traced
That in the life Omnipotent lie based?
  Or earth-grown atom's bounded soul
  Grasp the universal whole?

"The more he chafes, the worse his fetter galls
The luckless captive closed in dungeon walls,
And fighting chains and stones, he fighting falls.

Nor will that wasteful immolation
Touch his lofty victor's station.

"Woe be to him perverse, who, weak and blind,
In pride refusing to behold, shall find
The ponderous roll of circumstance will grind
    His steps; and if he turn not, must
    Bruise and crush him into dust.

"We are the Lord's, not ours, His angels sing;
So you, mine own, bow meekly to your King,
And striving hard and long His grace will bring:
    His voice shall through the battle cry,
    When the strife is raging high."

She fluttering paused: awhile her surging zeal
All utterance overwhelmed to mute appeal:
I felt as men who fallen in battle feel,
    When far their chief's sword, like a gem,
    Points to glory not for them.

"When naked heaven is azure to your eyes,
And light shines everywhere, you can be wise;
But, when its storms in common course arise,
    To you the wind but sobs and grieves
    Wailing with the streaming leaves.

"Rust eats the steel, and moths corrupt the cloth,
And peevish doubts destroy the soul that's loth
To strive for duty, merged in shameful sloth,
    And lolls a weary wretch forlorn,
    While men reap the mellow corn.

"It is not man's to dream in sweet repose;
He toils and murmurs, as he wondering goes,
Poor changeful glitter on the stream that flows
    In lapses huge and solemn roar,
    Ever on without a shore.

"The plantlet grown in darkness puts forth spray;
Through loaded gloom yearns feebly toward some ray
Of bounty golden from the outer day
    That shines eternally sublime
    On the dancing motes of time."

The music stopped, and passed into a smile
Of tenderness, which she impressed to guile
Her pain from me: I gazed as one awhile

Escaped, who sees twin rainbows shine
O'er his wrecked ship gulfed in brine.

My lost soul sank adown in soundless seas
To ruined heaps besprent with ancient lees
Of wealth: by soft stupendous ocean-trees;
   By anchors forged in early time,
   Changed to trails of rusted slime:

To where, what seemed a tomb, in this deep hell
Of night, bore a dim name I dread to tell:
And there I heard sound some gigantic bell,
   Whose thunder laughing through my brain
   Mocked me back to flesh again.

Here all was emptier than the empty shade
Of mist before a midnight moon decayed:
Here life was strange as death, and more dismayed
   My spirit, now scarce conscious she
   Urged entreaty yet to me.

"'Tis life in life to know the King is just,
And will not animate his helpless dust
With fire unquenchable whose ardour must
   Achieve majestic deeds that raise
   Universal shouts of praise:

"Shouts of acclaim that gather into story,
Chanted by one on some high promontory
Who glowing in the dawn's advancing glory,
   Far down upon the listening crowd
   Shines through swathes of lingering cloud:

"And fires, by what he sings, to noble feud
With grosser instincts, the charged multitude,
That grow in temper and similitude
   To those great souls whose victories
   Triumph still in melodies:

"This fire will not be granted to distress,
To fail in cold dead ash and bitterness:
He will not grant true love that yearns to bless
   The world, that it may only sigh
   Back into itself and die."

The words here faltering sank to undertone:
Her soul was murmuring to itself alone
On some wide desolation, dark, unknown;

Whose limits, stretched from mortal sight
Touch the happy hills of light.

"I, toiling at the task assigned to me,
Am summoned from my labour suddenly:
The King recalls his handmaiden; and she
  Submissively herself anoints,
  Going whither He appoints.

"The sheaves are garnered now, her work is done,
The day is waning, and she must be gone,
To bend herself before the Holy One,
  And strictly her appointed meed
  There accept in very deed."

Dead silence, more than if a thunder-stroke
Had crashed the summer air, my sense awoke
To sudden apprehension: hard the yoke
  Of misery was mine to bear;
  Wrath-befooled, in my despair

I went, and, leaning from the lattice, mused
On my immeasurable woe; accused
Heaven's King, that, like an earthly king, abused
  His power omnipotent, and hurled
  Curses broadcast on the world.

Then glancing toward her danger thought, "A cell
Of noxious vapours this dull life; as well
She should escape: so pure! she scarce could dwell
  With sinful creatures who alway
  Stumbling take the stain of clay

"But I unworthy! How in conscience I—
How could I hazard guidance in her high
Cold path of duty leading to the sky!
  As well hold torch to light a star
  Shining, mystic, nebular.

"She yearns to bless the world: just love for all
Best shows in love for one; love cannot fall
Like sunshine over half this wondrous ball,
  But her impulses yearn to bless
  All the world. Strange tenderness!"

This shameful mockery of myself alone
Was interrupted by a sobbing moan
That brought me to her coach, where low mine own

Sweet Love lay swooning ashy white,
    Eyelids closing from the light.

Ah, coarse, hard, bitter, brutal self! A beast
In passion, nay far worse than such, to feast
On baseless anger against her whose least
    Stray word was kind; her daily food
    Interest in another's good.

My passion then, like an unruly horse
Checked by a master's hand, fell slack; its force
Unnerved, and stifling me with hot remorse;
    Frightened, despairing, "Love," I cried,
    Wildly busy at her side;

And kissed and chafed her brow; I chafed her hand;
Audacious grown with fear, released the band
That clasped her tender waist, and keenly scanned
    Each feature, till her opening eyes
    Met my own in bright surprise

"Ah you! I had from you passed and the world
Through endless nothing rudely was I hurled
While you there hung above, your proud lip curled,
    Regarding me with piercing hate
    Crying I deserved my fate."

We met each other, as when waters meet
In long continued shock, and muttering, sweet
Confusion mixed in unity complete
    That changing time may not dissever;
    One in love and one for ever.

Purged by remorse, love knit my strength; and now
Came gracious power to still upon her brow
Those troubled waves of some dark underflow;
    Her soul victorious over pain
    Spoke in golden smiles again.

We sat and read how Prospero closed his strife
With evil, wrought his charm, and crowned his life
In making two fair beings man and wife:
    Of brave Count Gismond's happy lot;
    And the Lady of Shalott.

We ceased; for eve had come by dusky stealth.
I saw, while lifting her, like crimson health
Burn in her cheeks, holding the weighted wealth

Of all the worlds in heaven to me;
Held her long, long, lingeringly:

And laying down more than my life, her weight;
Scarce kissed her pallid hands, then moved with great
Reluctance, bodeful, from her placid state;
   But, ere my slow feet reached the door,
   Turned and caught one last look more,

And awe-struck stood to see portentous loom
From her large eyes full gazing through the gloom
Love darkly wedded to eternal doom,
   As she were gazing from the dead:
   Falling at her feet I said,

"Bless me, dear Love, bless me before I go;
With love divine a beam of comfort throw,
For guidance and support, that I through woe
   Be raised and purified in grace
   Worthy to behold your face."

She bowed her head in stately tenderness
Low whispering as her hands my brow did press,
"I pray that He will your lone spirit bless,
   And if to leave you be my fate,
   Pray you for me while I wait."

A useless pang in her no more to wake,
I forced myself away, nor dared to take
Another look for her beloved sake;
   My face had told of the distressed
   Swollen heart labouring in my breast.

When in the outer air, I felt as one
Fresh startled from a dream, wherein the sun
Had dying left the earth a dingy, dun
   Annihilation. The nightjar
   Only thrilled the air afar:

No other sound was there: a muffled breeze
Crept in the shrubs, and shuddered up the trees,
Then sought the ghost-white vapour of the leas,
   Where one long sheet of dismal cloud
   Swathed the distance in a shroud.

A solitary eye of cold stern light
Stared threateningly beyond the Western height,
Wrapped in the closing shadows of the night;

And all the peaceful earth had slept
But that eye stern vigil kept.

I wandered wearily I knew not where;
Up windy downs far-stretching, bleak and bare;
Through swamps that soddened under stagnant air;
  In blackest woods and brambled mesh,
  Thorny bushes tore my flesh:

Amid the ripening corn I heard it sigh,
Hollow and sad, as night crawled sluggishly:
Hollow and sadly sighed the corn while I
  Moved darkly in the midst, a blight
  Darkening more the hateful night.

My soul its hoarded secrets emptied on
The vaulted gloom of night: old fancies shone,
And consecrated ancient hopes long gone;
  Old hopes that long had ceased to burn,
  Gone, and never to return.

No starlight pierced the dense vault over head,
And all I loved was passing or had fled:
So on I wandered where the pathway led;
  And wandered till my own abode
  Spectral pale rose from the road.

What time I gained my home I saw the morn
Made dimly on the sullen East. Wayworn
I went into the echoing house forlorn,
  Heartsick and weary sought my room,
  Better had it been my tomb.

I lay, and ever as my lids would close
In dull forgetfulness to slumberous doze,
Lone sounds of phantom tolling scared repose;
  Till wearied nature, sore oppressed,
  Slowly sank and dropped to rest.

X. WILL-O'-THE-WISP

  "Gone the sickness, fled the pain,
  Health comes bounding back again,
And all my pulses tingle for delight.
  Together what a pleasant thing
  To ramble while the blackbirds sing,

And pasture lands are sparkling dewy bright!

"Soon will come the clear spring weather,
Hand in hand we'll roam together,
And hand in hand will talk of springs to come;
As on the morning when you played
The necromancer with my shade,
In senseless shadow gazing darkly dumb.

"Cast away that cloudy care,
Or, I vow, in my parterre
You shall not enter when the lilies blow,
And I go there to stand and sing
Songs to the heaven-white wondrous ring;
Sir Would-be-Wizard of the crumpled brow!"

XI. GIVEN OVER

The men of learning say she must
Soon pass and be as if she had not been.
To gratify the barren lust
Of Death, the roses in her cheeks are seen
To blush so brightly, blooming deeper damascene.

All hope and doubt, all fears are vain:
The dreams I nursed of honouring her are past,
And will not comfort me again.
I see a lurid sunlight throw its last
Wild gleam athwart the land whose shadows lengthen fast.

It does not seem so dreadful now
The horror stands out naked, stark, and still:
I am quite calm, and wonder how
My terror played such mad pranks with my will.
The North winds fiercely blow, I do not feel them chill.

All things must die: somewhere I read
What wise and solemn men pronounce of joy;
No sooner born, they say, than dead:
The strife of being, but a whirling toy
Humming a weary moan spun by capricious boy.

Has my soul reached a starry height
Majestically calm? No monster, drear
And shapeless, glares me faint at night;
I am not in the sunshine checked for fear

That monstrous shapeless thing is somewhere crouching near?

   No; woe is me! far otherwise:
The naked horror numbs me to the bone;
   In stupor calm its cold blank eyes
Set hard at mine. I do not fall or groan,
Our island Gorgon's face had changed me into stone.

XII. STORM

Now thickening round the shrunken baseless sky,
   Sullen vapours crawl
Climbing to masses, tumbled heavily
   Grim in giant sprawl,
That smother up domed heaven's scud-fleckered height
And form like mortal armies ranged for fight.

This lighted gloom spreads ghastly on the land;
   Sheep do crowd; and herds
Collecting, bellow pitifully bland.
   Quiet are the birds
In ghostly trees that shiver not a sound:
And leaves decayed drop straight unto the ground.

Drearily solemn runs a monotone,
   Heard through breathless hush,
Swollen torrents hissing far in lavish moan,
   Foamed with headlong rush,
Sob on protesting, toward annihilation,
Their solitary dismal lamentation.

This gloom has sucked all interest from the scene,
   Now changed wrathful grey:
Familiar things, that staring plain had been,
   Fade in mists away:
At ambush, watching from its stormy lair,
Some danger hovering loads the stagnant air.

It serves to little purpose I may know
   That electric law
Whereby the jagged glare and thunder-blow
   Latent impulse draw;
No less my danger. Ha! that lightning flash
Proclaims in fire the coming thunder-crash.

But what care I though deluges down pour

Beating earth to mire,
Though heaven shattering with the thunder's roar
 Scorcheth now in fire,
Though every planet molten from its place
Should trickle lost through everlasting space;

For this blank prospect, void of all but dread,
 Void as any tomb,
My soul has left; and by a lonely bed,
 In a girl's sick room,
Hangs there expectant of her parting breath,
The silent voice of doom, the stroke of death.

PART THE SECOND

I. MY LADY IN DEATH

All is but coloured show. I look
 Into the green light shed
 By leaves above my head,
And feel its inmost worth forsook
 My being, when she died.
 This heart, now hot and dried,
Halts, as the parched course where a brook
 Mid flowers was wont to flow,
 Because her life is now
No more than stories in a printed book.

Grass thickens proudly o'er that breast,
 Clay-cold and sadly still,
 My happy face felt thrill.
How much her dear, dear mouth expressed!
 And now are closed and set
 Lips which my own have met!
Her eyelids by the damp earth pressed!
 Damp earth weighs on her eyes;
 Damp earth shuts out the skies.
My Lady rests her heavy, heavy rest.

To see her high perfection sweep
 The favoured earth, as she
 With welcoming palms met me!
How can I but recall and weep?
 Her hands' light charm was such,
 Care vanished at their touch.
Her feet spared little things that creep;

"For stars are not," she'd say,
  "More wonderful than they."
And now she sleeps her heavy, heavy sleep.

Immortal hope shone on that brow,
  Above whose waning forms
  Go softly real worms.
Surely it was a cruel blow
  Which cut my Darling's life
  Sharply, as with a knife;
I hate my own that lets me grow
  As grows a bitter root
  From which rank poisons shoot
Upon the grave where she is lying low.

Ah, hapless fate! Could it be just,
  That her young life should play
  Its easy, natural way;
Then, with an unexpected thrust,
  Be hence thus rudely sent;
  Even as her feelings blent
With those around, whose love would trust
  Her willing power to bless,
  For all their happiness?
Alone she moulders into common dust.

Small birds twitter and peck the weeds
  That wave above this bed
  Where my dear Love lies dead:
They flutter and burst the globed seeds,
  And beat the downy pride
  Of dandelions, wide:
From speargrass, bowed with watery beads,
  The wet uniting, drips
  In sparkles off the tips:
In mallow bloom the wild bee drops and feeds.

No more she hears, where vines adorn
  Her window, on the boughs
  Birds chirrup an arouse:
Flies, buzzing, strengthening with the morn,
  She will not hear again
  At random strike the pane:
No more against the newly shorn
  Grass edges will her gown
  In playful waves be thrown,
As she walks forth to view what flowers are born.

Nor ponder more those dark green rings
  Stained quaintly on the lea,
  To picture elfin glee;
While through the grass a faint air sings,
  And swarms of insects revel
  Along the sultry level:
No more will watch their brilliant wings,
  Now lightly dip, now soar,
  Then sink, and rise once more.
My Lady's death makes dear these trivial things.

One noon, within an oak's broad shade,
  Lost in delightful talk,
  We rested from our walk.
Beyond the shadow, large and staid,
  Cows chewed with drowsy eye
  Their cud complacently:
Elegant deer walked o'er the glade,
  Or stood with wide bright eyes
  Gazing a short surprise;
And up the fern slope nimble conies played.

As rooks cawed labouring through the heat;
  Each wing-flap seemed to make
  Their weary bodies ache;
And swallows, though so wildly fleet,
  Made breathless pauses there
  At something in the air.
All disappeared: our pulses beat
  Distincter throbs, and each
  Turned and kissed without speech,
She trembling from her mouth down to her feet.

Then, as I felt her bosom heave,
  And listened to the din
  Of joyous life within,
Could I but in my heaven believe,
  Assured by that repose
  Within my heart, and those
Warm arms around my neck! While eve
  In shadowy silence came
  And quenched the Western flame,
That lingered round her as if loth to leave.

Then told I in a whispered tone
  Of that approaching time,
  When merry peal and chime
Of marriage ringing should make known,

In crashes through the air
  Exultingly we were
By solemn rite each other's own:
  And she, confiding, meek,
  Against mine pressed her cheek,
And gave response in happy tears alone.

No heed of time took we, because
  Those clanging bells had quite
  Absorbed us in delight.
A happiness so perfect awes
  The failing pulse and breath,
  Like the mute doom of death:
Then, in an instantaneous pause
  Flashed on my vacant eye
  A swift Eternity;
And starting, as if clutched by demon-claws,

Awakened from a dizzy swoon,
  I felt appalling fears
  With ringings in my ears,
And wondered why the glaring moon
  Swung round the dome of night
  With such stupendous might.
Next came, like the sweet air of June,
  A treacherous calm suspense
  That bred a loathly sense,
Some nameless ill would overwhelm us soon.

She passed like summer flowers away.
  Her aspect and her voice
  Will never more rejoice,
For she lies hushed in cold decay.
  Broken the golden bowl
  Which held her hallowed soul:
It was an idle boast to say
  "Our souls are as the same,"
  And stings me now to shame:
Her spirit went, and mine did not obey.

The black truth, with a fiery dart,
  Went hurtling through my thought,
  When I beheld her brought
Whence she with life did not depart.
  Her beauty by degrees
  Sank, sharpened from disease:
The heavy sinking at her heart
  Sucked hollows in her cheek,

And made her eyelids weak,
Though oft they opened wide with sudden start.

The Deathly Power in silence drew
  My Lady's life away.
  I watched, dumb for dismay,
The shock of thrills that quivered through
  Her wasted frame, and shook
  The meaning in her look,
As near, more near, the moment grew.
  O horrible suspense!
  O giddy impotence!
I saw her features lax, and change their hue.

Her gaze, grown large with fate, was cast
  Where my mute agonies
  Made sadder her sad eyes:
Her breath caught with short plucks and fast,
  Then one hot choking strain;
  She never breathed again.
I had the look which was her last:
  Her love, when breath was gone,
  One moment lingering shone,
Then slowly closed, and hope for ever passed.

A dreadful tremour ran through space
  When first the mournful toll
  Rang for My Lady's soul.
The shining world was hell; her grace
  Only the flattering gleam
  And mockery of a dream:
Oblivion struck me like a mace,
  And as a tree that's hewn
  I dropped, in a dead swoon,
And lay a long time cold upon my face.

Earth had one quarter turned before
  My miserable fate
  Pressed down with its whole weight.
My sense came back; and shivering o'er
  I felt a pain to bear
  The sun's keen cruel glare,
Which shone not warm as heretofore;
  And never more its rays
  Will satisfy my gaze:
No more; no more; O, never any more.

II. DAY DREAM

What art thou whispering lowly to thy babe,
O wan girl-mother, with Madonna lids
Downcast? Why pressest thou so close his pale
Geranium cheek to thy yet whiter breast?
Ah, doubtless sweet; to feel him draw the stream
That fills with strength his lily limbs! And laughs
Thine own heart with his deeply dimpled laughter,
Answering straight thy dainty finger's touch?
And understandeth he that murmurous moan,
Wherewith thou hushest, patting him to rest?

What visions charm thy gaze, now resting wide
In settled sweet content? Beholdest thou
Thy babe, now sprung a man, walk sunhazed slopes
With one lovelier than visions; lovely as
The truth, O Love, when thou dost smile on me?
Or seest thou him still greater grown in might,
And stout of action marching on to reach
That changeful coloured flag, whose waving crests
The glittering heights of fame, for which men pant;
Unmindful there what tempests rage and sweep;
Alas; what dream has made that watery veil
Hide thine eye's light from mine; even as a mist
Passing between me and a harvest moon!
And whence this shadowy wall that baulks my gaze?
Why fadest thou, thyself, in mist, O Love?
Whither hath fled thy babe—and where art thou?—
Where am I?—Is it life—a dream—or death?

Ah me; alas, this crushing wretchedness!
And I a vainer fool than one who yearns
Clutching at rainbows spanned across the sky!
Ah, hope diseased! My spirit lured astray
By siren hope drifts hard by some dark fate:
And hope alternating despair has mixed
My life so long with charnelled death, that I
Can scarce resolve the present from my past,
Nor what might once have been from what is now.

Ah, Dearest! shall I never see thy face
Again: not ever; never any more?
I know that fancy was but naught, and one
Born of past hope: I know thy earthly form
Is mouldering in its tomb; but yet, O Love,
Thy spirit must dwell somewhere in this waste

Of worlds, that fill the overwhelming heavens
With light and motion; that could never die;
And wilt thou not vouchsafe one beaming look
To ease a lonely heart that beats in pain
For loss of thee, and only thee, O Love?
Or hast thou found in that pure life thou livest
My soul was an unworthy choice for thine,
And therefore takest no count of its despair?
And yet, yea verily, thy love was true;
I would not wrong thee with another thought:
I would not enter at the gates of heaven
By thinking else than that thy love was true.
But I obtain no response to my cries,
Making within my soul all void, and cold,
And comfortless.

      Ay, empty, as this grate,
Of life, wherefrom the fire has well nigh fled,
Leaving but chasmed ugliness and ruin:
And weak as faltering of these taper flames
Half sunken in their sockets, by whose gleam
I see, though faintly, where my books stand ranged
Most mute; though sometime eloquent to me;
And where my pictures hang with other forms
Instinct from what I know: where friends portrayed
Like ghosts loom on me from another world.
Then what remains, but, like a child worn out
With weeping, that I sink me down to rest,
To sleep, not dream—and if I could to die?

III. MY LADY'S VOICE FROM HEAVEN

I had been sitting by her tomb
  In torpor one dark night;
When fitful tremours shook the doom
Of cold lethargic settled gloom,
  That weighed upon my sight:

And while I sat, and sickly heaves
  Disturbed my spirit's sloth,
A wind came, blown o'er distant sheaves,
That hissing, tore and lashed the leaves
  And lashed the undergrowth:

It roared and howled, it raged about
  With some determined aim;

And storming up the night, brought out
The moon, that like a happy shout,
  Called forth My Lady's name,

In sudden splendour on the stone.
  Then, for an instant, I
Snatched and heaped up my past, bestrown
With hopes and kisses, struggling moan,
  And pangs: as suddenly,

Oppressed with overwhelming weight,
  Down fell the edifice;
When touched, as by the hand of Fate,
My gloom was gone. I felt my state
  So light, I sobbed for bliss.

The loud winds, spent in seeking rest,
  Dropped dead. My fevered brow
Drank coolness from the grass it pressed;
And in my desolated breast
  A change began to grow,

While feeling those tears slowly drain
  The load of grief which had
A sluggish curse within me lain,
Save when remembrance wrought my brain
  For vivid moments mad.

My tears, as treasures of a wreck
  That in the ocean slept,
Recovered, ran without a check;
And earth was my good mother's neck
  To which I clung and wept.

I rose at length, and felt a dense
  Benumbed dead weight. And now
The night air hung in deep suspense!
A singing hush that pressed my sense
  And stunned me like a blow:

Through my lids clenched the living air
  In gold and purple rings
Danced musically round me there,
The light it held throbbed with the glare
  And beat of rapid wings.

Mine eyes I dared not try to raise;
  My Lady's beamed on me

In fixed serenity of gaze,
And were what old sunshiny days
    In childhood used to be.

A gasping lapse; and I was whirled
    Round the faint void of space;
In dizzy circles hugely hurled,
I saw the constellated world
    With every orb embrace,

To one stupendous vortex-light,
    Spinning a fiery ram,
Then fail, struck out by sudden night;
When swung adown in headlong might,
    Earth's touch shook through my brain.

The dumb sound in mine ears was burst
    By her portentous voice;
As sweet as death to one accursed,
As unto one near blind for thirst
    A running water's noise.

Her voice in some translucent star,
    Remote, beyond my sight,
Was singing marvellously far;
And yet so strangely near to jar,
    As jars too strong a light.

She sang a song. She warbled low,
    She did not sing in words;
I felt it in my spirit glow,
And knew it, as with joy I know
    The morning shouts of birds.

But hard the task I undertake,
    With mortal tongue to reach
The utterance of my Love, and make
Her high immortal meaning break
    To clearness through my speech!

I can no more, with glimmering trope
    That into darkness runs,
Reveal its depth, than they could hope,
Who on in lifelong blindness grope,
    To sing of rising suns.

"Or e'er that life my King had lent
    Was lifted into rest,

His message through my lips He sent,
And on thy path His glory went
  To guide thee to the blessed.

"But thou didst turn thy face, and scorn
  His grace divine as nought;
And set thy gaze to earth forlorn,
And rage at fate, till gaunt and worn,
  Death mouldered in thy thought.

"Thou, blindly gross, didst toy with clay,
  And in the ghastly gleam
Of charnel gloom didst kiss decay;
And many full moons waned away,
  And left thee in thy dream.

"For with thy Lily's worldly dress
  Thou didst thine eyesight fill;
And scorn to know its loveliness
Were but an empty boast unless
  Made living by His will.

"Thou mourn'dst not most the vanished soul
  Which was my Lord's through thine;
But more the broken pleasure-bowl,
Whose golden richness shed, when whole,
  Its splendour in thy wine.

"And therefore living wert thou made
  To taste the cup of death;
And therefore did the glory fade,
From guidance into deadly shade
  That iced thy shuddering breath.

"Permitted, now I come to thee:
  I warn thee of thy sin;
I urge thee cleanse thine eyesight free,
That purified thy soul may see
  The way his love to win.

"His love incomprehensible
  Did never turn away
From penitent whom harm befell;
But springeth like a desert well
  For thirsting poor estray.

"Let him who scorneth mercy shown,
  Unhappy one, beware!

For whoso lives in pride alone,
His pride shall harden to a stone
  Too great for him to bear.

"And whoso, having warned been,
  Refuseth still to turn,
Behind his shadow, shrunken mean,
A poring spectre shall be seen
  With livid stare and girn.

"Thou troubled one, who unto me
  Art next my Lord's own grace,
O turn to Him, and He will be
A refuge from thy misery,
  A smile upon thy face!

"A righteous strength will nerve thine arm,
  And courage fill thy breast:
And having bravely warred on harm,
The cries of victory shall charm
  Thy dying eyes to rest.

"And succoured ones shall praise his name
  Who, toiling for them, died.
And, nobly sung, his honest fame
Shall beat in hearts unborn, and claim
  Their love and grateful pride.

"And Love will lead her sacrifice
  To where a shining row
Stand beckoning to the heights of bliss;
And she will clasp his hands and kiss
  Welcome upon his brow."

I knew not when the singing ceased
  To trance my brightened soul,
Then from that long eclipse released.
But looking hopeful towards the East,
  I saw flush pole to pole

The dawn, that had begun to show,
  And through dank vapour burned,
As in a sick face lying low
The rich incarnadine would glow,
  When healthy life returned.

Small drowsy chirping met the light,
  And dim in lowlands far

Lone marsh-birds winged their misty flight;
What time Her aspect on my sight
　Beamed from the morning star.

It waned into the warbling day;
　That, rising fierce and strong,
Now looked the Western gloom away,
And kindled such a roundelay,
　The world awoke with song,

And fresh delicious breezes came
　With scents of paradise
So tingling through my knitted frame,
That never since I lisped a name
　Knew I such joy arise.

Pure was the azure over head;
　Bright was the earth around;
While I on resolution fed,
And moved, as one called from the dead,
　In silence on the ground.

Toward my home I walked, elate
　With hope and settled plan:
And reverent to the will of Fate,
In every step I trod my weight,
　A sober-minded man.

PART THE THIRD

I. YEARS AFTER

Our world has spun ten circles round the light
Since here she vanished. In my helpless gaze,
To mark the spot, was fixed this carven stone,
Raw, garish, stolidly obtrusive then,
Now harmonising kindly with the rest.
A spray of centipedal ivy creeps
From death to birth, and reaches to her name;
With kisslike touch its tender leaflets feel
The letter's edge,—I scarce can think it chance.

Now scene by scene that strange old long-ago,
Crowding my opened memory, presents
Tumultuous, as in dreams, some dreadful state
Wherein I knew not falsehood from the truth;

Where hope ascending struck the star of Love,
Then fell down headlong grovelling in despair;
But rose at length and walked the beaten way.
So dim and far these things; so worn and changed,
I scarcely feel that I am he who sought
And won her love. And is it true indeed,
That I absorbed in tenderest intercourse
Of trustful glance, and trustful clasping hands,
With her went wandering by the river side;
While over head melodious branches sang,
Scattering the gold of sunset-dazzled flowers
Breathing their perfumed sweetness from our path,
That flickering went to where in purple woods
The rugged church tower burned a wall of fire!

Did I, when silence awed the winter woods,
And giant shadows trenched the frosty ground
From bole and limb whose vault held in the night,
Love to behold the full-grown magic moon
Cast splendour glittering on the silver rime?

Yes; mid the notes and emerald flush of spring,
With swollen brooks exulting through the fields,
And rainy wind that in an ocean-roar
Bore down the forest tops the livelong day,
Through straggling gleams, through random wafts of shade,
Rejoicingly I trod the glistening paths.

Yes, I it was, in dreamy golden haze,
Beheld poor men hard toiling all the hours,
And thought them happier than the birds that sang,
That sang and trilled in gurgles of delight.

Dallying I loitered in the golden time
Long after the loved nightingale had ceased
To pour his passionate impulse over plains
Of shivering corn, now ripened into wealth;
When sunset-coloured fruit in orchard crofts
Hung slowly mellowing under azure noons;
And, hushed in darkened leaves, the dreaming air
Swelled gently to a whispering sound, and died.
With joy I wandered on from knoll to knoll
And lost in marvel, drank the lisping winds,
The fairy winds that lisped me all was good.
Nor marked I when the clogged horizon flew
In dusky vapour crowding up the skies;
But woke anon when deathlike pallor thrown
From wrathful drift laid the whole land in gloom;

When war, enormous war, broke through the heavens,
In sheets and streaking fire and thunderous clap,
With shock on shock, that crushed the ripened corn,
And swept the piled up midsummer to ruin.
That wrenched great timbers of a thousand years,
Shaking the strong foundations of the land.
And when at last the terrible tempest fell,
Wide heaven was emptied of the sun and stars,
And void of more than all their light to me.

Like fretted me to hollow weariness
When my sweet Dove of Paradise went off,
Ascending, glory-guarded, into heaven.
Then feeding on the past, and fondling death,
I grew in livid horror: soon had grown,
By foul self cankered, to a charnel ghoule,
Had not Almighty God, gracious in love,
Permitted her own presence once again,
Mysterious as a vision, yet once more
To come a shining warning and reveal
Athwart my path unfathomable gulfs,
And kindle hope wherewith I still might gain
The hills that shine for ever to the blessed.

Much striving has been mine since those events
Ruled the pulsation of my daily life:
And now they are a vulgar chronicle,
And gossiped over by the rudest tongues.
A haunting song of old felicities
Lured me, scarce consciously, down here to muse
Upon my shattered dreams; safe from the roar
Of interests in our grim metropolis,
The beating heart of England and the world.
Not seen by me, since on that wondrous night
Her consolation came into my soul;
Yet here again I stand beside her tomb—
And here I muse, more wise and not so sad.

Hers was a gracious and a gentle house!
Rich in obliging nice observances
And famed ancestral hospitality.
A cool repose lay grateful through the place;
And pleasant duties promptly, truly done,
And every service moved by hidden springs
Sped with intelligence, went smoothly round.

The steward to that stately country home
Looked native there as lichen to the oak.

He first held station, chief in care and trust,
That day which gave his baby mistress birth;
And her he loved as father loves his own,
Bearing her too that reverence which we feel
Toward those who, born to loftier state than ours,
Sit their high fortune with becoming grace.
His love she ever sumptuously returned
In bounteous thankfulness for service done:
How brightly twinkled then his shrewd grey eyes,
And shone the roundness where his honest cheeks
Played to the rippling gladness of his mouth!
In childhood rambles, it was mostly he
She chose for partner, spite of blandishment;
And to her winsome ways he would forego
His pompous surveillance of wine and plate,
To guard her, lilting, where the summer lay
On honeyed murmuring limes, and under elms,
August with knotted centuries of strength
And rooks sonorous in their shadowy heights.
By thymy slopes, foot-deep in sward they roved,
Both lightly garrulous, and she, sweet child,
Fusing her whole attention into joy,
Until they stood before the lake, that gleamed
With water-lilies, sun, and moving cloud.
Then straight the flanking sedge, and reeds remote,
Gave clattering ducks and wild outlandish fowl,
That tore in stormy scampering and splash
To snap with clamour at the crumbled bread,
He had provided slyly, bent on fun:
The swans meanwhile, majestic, puffed, and slow,
Came proudly into action; but alas,
To small result; for by mischance the spoil
Through dexterous skirmish fell to meaner bills.
"Our bread is all cast on the waters now,
And well I'd like to know how many days
It must bide there before 'tis found again!" —
Some fool's dull joke repeated: good man, he,
Unversed in deep text comment, never dreamed
What time its Abyssinian mountain roots
Swollen by fresh torrents mixed in Nubian lands,
And thundered down from rocky ledge to ledge;
How sacred Nilus flooding bank and plain
Transformed old Egypt to a shining sea:
And slaves in swarthy crowds, despised as dirt,
Paddled upon the water scattering corn,
While swam to their sad eyes a raking glance
Of temple sphinxes, palms, and pyramids,
Faint sacrificial fire with dismal cries;

And small hard masters, armed with blooded thongs,
Jocose and fierce, scourged out their utmost toil.
Long ages ere man heard this promised hope,
THE FIRST SHALL BE THE LAST, THE LAST THE FIRST.
But the dear child his vacant prattle heard
In wonder, and believed it lore profound:
And ever after, when in solemn church,
(The very church I have before me now!)
Or household prayer, these words were touched upon,
Pert visions would intrude of gabbling fowls
Mid splashing water, sedge, and lily stars.

In wending home, he filled her lap with flowers;
And she, ere yet the house was reached, unloosed
His guarding hand, ran forward, glinted through
The porch, and with a joyous outcry lit
The room, where sat in converse or at books
Her parents: then, as she an hour before
Had seen those mirrored marvels of the lake
All trembling merge to one confused turmoil
Of beauty broken into shattered light,
When o'er its surface swept the hungry fowls,
So blurred with shifting catches, so involved
Through eagerness, her babbled narrative
To the kind mother, who, embracing her,
Felt satisfied her child had been well pleased.
Then the great father, he would lightly lift
To knee his darling girl; with fingers cup
The tiny chin, and kiss the rosebud mouth;
And gently his large tawny hand would stroke
That woven sunshine glowing down her back,
Which changed to deepest auburn glossed with gold,
Calling her tricksy names. But, when at length
Appeared the calm inevitable nurse,
He laughed; and she in screaming laughter flew
By stalwart arm thrust high above his head
Immeshed in wild flowers emptied from her lap,
Which shaking off, he brought the screamer down,
And gaily swung her into willing arms.
She talked these childhood memories while we strolled
Among the scenes which bred them; for she loved
To dwell on things which some regard as slight:
But in her presence, told by her own self,
With clear apt words and satisfying voice;
The violet poise of her most graceful head
Flung forth in lighted gesture to reveal
The very fact; her hovering white hand
Almost in music warbling with her words,

And bounding all the tenderest care to please;—
Now, one by one, these aits of memory glow
In hallowed splendour, and have made less dark
A life I feel not altogether vain.

So common was her mother's lot, that who
Can say "Like is not mine" is blessed indeed:
For they are countless that on shades have thrown
Their passion had been chilled for evermore!
Scarce at her bloom, and years before she met
The destined man her husband, girl-like she
Adored a youth with sparkling genius graced,
Who bound on great adventure spread all sail;
But needed ballast, working common sense,
And meeting storms, he foundered and was lost.
For long his fate dragged at her heart; it drained
Her strength; it left her vague and desolate:
Her life became as chill uneasy dreams
Wherefrom we cannot break. Yet be it said,
Lowly and truly gentle were her ways;
She was a tender and obedient wife,
And in a sweet and plaintive graciousness
Her every act performed. I trust her mind,
Subdued by constant sadness unavowed,
Grew clear of shadows, and at last could dwell
Upon the future, that in one straight path
Reached Justice throned in everlasting light,
And learned to feel that chastisement is love.

Somewhat through lethargy; and partly sense
Of duty in forgetfulness of grief;
With pleadings due to her own kindliness,
She came to take another as her lord;
Then came to yield herself in all and wed
Her husband's own indomitable will:
He having gained her, cherished her, and loved
Her mild compliance with the strength of life.

He was a man of thews and goodly frame
Made swart in battle. Under Indian suns
Our foes had often there been taught to know
That weight of arm, resistless when he closed
Charging upon them with his sword and eye.
But when his father died, he left the East
For England; here to rule his own estate,
And reign among the county gentlemen,
Who duly came with pride to own him chief.
He had the kingly look of born command,

An eagle set of eye and curve of neck;
A cutting insight backed by solid sense;
Vast knowledge, and the facile use of it,
To break obstruction, or direct the force
Of will resolved to compass every end.
Withal a broad and generous natured man
Who ever kindly turned the doubtful scale
Against himself: no tenant ever mourned
The day when the new master came to rule;
Nor were old village gossips heard lament
The good times fled with their departed lord.

Culture went hand in hand with strength in him:
Broad-versed was he in science; rock and soil,
Plant, shell, bird, beast, to complex form of man,
With something of the stars. Historic works
He mostly read; and ofttimes dug for trace
Of steps long past in archaeology.
He loved the singers of our native land
Who take our souls up to the worth of life;
And those deep thinkers whose conclusions show
The secret principles that work the world.
He prized laborious Hallam; but declared
Carlyle half mad; "A coil of restive thoughts,
That touch on nothing sound or practical,
Told in outrageous jargon, cumbersome
As any Laplander's costume!" Which I
In ruffled pride would always straight oppose,
"Sound or unsound, his word is daylight truth,
That breeding heroes once was England's boast,
And now we brag of making millionaires.
Your 'practical' means shortest cut to wealth:
But far too frequently purse robs the heart;
One growing heavy drains the other dry.
His style, poetically pregnant, oft
By note of admiration merely, hints
More than crammed Pro Con of your favourite's page."
At this he shouts a scornful roaring laugh,
The table shaking, and the vessels chinked
As fell his weighty arm: with massive gaze
In hurly-burly sort he bantered me:
"Young bubble-dreamer, plotting stanza rhymes,
What can you know of laws: what know of plans
Which bound these varied interests of ours,
Through crossing currents, fixed for certain ends,
To frame this state we call society,
The full outcome of immemorial time?
Know, here on earth wealth must not be despised,

For we are as we are. While men subsist
By interchanging goods and service, gold
Will be the grease that smooths the whole machine.
I grant a few, the greatest, live content
To give forth what has ripened in their minds;
But greed alone brings each result to grow
And spread its uses through the mass. Beside
Where honour, reason, or instinctive life,
Quite fails, there gold will prick the sluggard loon.
It wakes the drowsy lounger of the East,
Who lolls in sunshine idle as a gourd,
To toil like Irish hodmen. Roused, he hears
Coin ringing lively music; falls to work,
And digs, and hews, and grinds: he sees, not far,
Himself, a chief of horsemen richly clad,
Armed with long spears and silver-halted blades,
Seizing pachalic power by a swift blow.
But labour, having brought him gold, brings fears.
The weight of wealth has made his footfall staid;
He longs for order, settled government,
And stands, a stern upholder, by the law.

"I know you flout this 'gold materialism,'
For what you call the 'gold of evening skies:'
But let me tell you, boy, for you 'tis well
My lands are broad and bankers true, or else
Your maiden, she, poor girl, I often think,
Would want a crust to eat and shoes to wear."
Thus he, in what I call his 'copper-gilt,'
For which I paid him tinsel; "She want shoes!
Her feet will press the flowers of paradise,
And, being angel, she will need no food."
"Eugh! Get your tackle, let us catch some trout."

She never stayed a long while from her home,
But lived a quiet life; contentedly
Taking the continent and many things
On trust; feeling our landscapes satisfied
Her love for scenes. When from a visit she
Returned, no lovelier picture ever blessed
My sight than when she swam into his arms,
And stood in beauty, frail, against his strength
Supporting her, and kissed his lips and cheeks
And brow. He then, as if his daughter yet
Were but a child, would press the upturned head
Between his hands, where peered the innocent face
Rosy with smile and blush, like a sweet flower
Bursting its tawny sheath: whereon he gazed

A father's gaze immeasurably kind;
And long, in tenderness akin to pity,
There held her, who was beautiful and good.
One eve full late in balmy summer time
We feared the wind breathing of night had chilled
Her tranquil mother, as we paced a walk
Leading espalier-trellised to the house;
She ever heedful parted silently,
And flushed with sunset vanished from our gaze;
But we beheld her soon dawn from the porch
In haste bringing her mother's mantle. When,
As comes the tide-wave up an easy beach,
Played with a billowy sound and look of foam
The thousand folds round her advancing feet,
Her shape divine looking as great as ocean's
Light beyond: yet no sea bird that gleams
From the blue-arched illimitable heaven
Could glide with lightness airier than she
To hang the garment round her mother's neck;
And then strike, womanlike, the folds in place;
Kissing the thankful lips, and deftly fix
The fastening at her throat. While pondering thus
And patching these rich fragments, strange it seems
What little things obtrude on my regard!
I now remember every sculptured group,
And painted scene, and portrait, figured vase,
Each print unique, and gem, we once beheld
When visiting a mansion near, enriched
By generations of collected Art:
The masters, by whose hands the works were wrought,
Long mouldered into dust. Ah, well I know
Why some have burned their symbols in my brain
And rise before me now!

     Stone-bound, Narcissus
Droops melting in himself; and Echo by,
In shrunk despair, hangs envying what he wastes.
Through smouldering morning mists a glorious sun
The mountain-shoulder burns; above, transmutes
The zenith cloudlets into airy gold;
And deep down, seen through pure crystalline blue,
Glimmer the village, lake, and mountain range.
Superb at ease a Lady stands and smiles
Sweet welcome to the world: though centuries
Have lapsed since she approved her painter's work,
Her smile has such sincerity, all feel
They must have known her some time in their lives.
Here bossed on silver vase, a marriage train

Moves round to music: lookers-on cast flowers
Before the timid bending bride: meanwhile,
Stalwart and proud, her bridegroom smiles abroad
As at a dazzling sun: the pipers blow,
The harpers twang, the cymbals clash, youths sing;
Six maidens walk behind to hold her veil,
One pair are sad, the next look vain, and two
Prettily whisper secrets to themselves.
Here from old paper stands, and looks of men
The manliest, and king of English kings,
The lion Cromwell, in his dress of war:
Beneath him coils a monster welling blood,
Whose severed heads stretch round in scattered gleam
Of mitre jewelled, coronet and crown.
Sharp cut on gem, set in a thick gold ring,
The size and roundness of a lady's nail,
Love bleeding on the dart himself doth point;
Who thus had died, had not with tenderest touch
Immortal Psyche held the anguished heart
Fast to her own, and purified the pain,
And fanned him with her wings.

      And now, as then,
Along those hushed rich corridors we moved,
Poring each masterpiece we favoured most,
And would no longer stay, but felt some chance
Must serve us for the rest: musing, I pass
From scene to scene of My Dear Lady's life,
And leave my other memories undisturbed.

Beneath this airy sapphire's brooding rest,
Its shadows overcast me with a chill
Like coming storm, that black calamity
Which struck and took our Darling from their charge
And mine. Grief stupefied us all. At once
The childless mother lost her wavering strength,
And lay prostrated; never tasting life
On earth again! Beside her husband sat
And watched her fading; saw the last poor smile
Wane from her features; till the closing eyes
Lit into tearful rapture; when he knew
Love's immortality to her revealed.
With both her own she mutely clasped his hand,
And held it in most gentle pressures fixed:
But when the tender grasp relaxed and fell,
The world closed round him to a stony blank.

And now was stricken down the mighty man;

As the ripe harvest levelled by a storm
At morningtide; which, ere sun warmth anew
Can flatter into strength, a second storm
O'erwhelms and scattereth to waste at even.

When that torpidity which follows pain
Through strangeness passed to natural regard
For daily wants; his vacant home he loathed:
His spacious garden grounds; his lake; his woods;
The breezy air; the overhanging heaven,
He loathed: he loathed them all. When spring aroused
The amorous songsters of the copse and field
To seasonable joy, their music mocked
His sadness with its echoes, babbling tales
Of what had been: and he, in bitterness,
Resolved to quit a place where every turn
Stood like a foe, whose settled leering eye
In silence gloared with hope to mark his fall;
He left our country. Far, in Eastern climes,
His nation serving well, he fought and died:
And never had a nobler man upheld
The majesty of England's worth and name.

Long toil-devoted years have gloomed and shone
Since these events closed up my doors of life.
Partly from choice, and part necessity,
With constancy have I sustained and urged
The work it was my duty to advance.
For, when my vision cleared again, I looked
And saw how mean a thing was man, who used
The produce of his fellows' energies
And gave back nothing.

        Then my spirit saw
This Island race two thousand years ago
In simple savagery, controlled by priests
More fell and bloody than the wolves that howled
At midnight round their monstrous altar-stones,
Scenting the sacrificial human blood.
Saw girt with legions lynx-eyed Caesar come
To taste of Briton's valour. When appeared
Legions succeeding legions, and the swarms
Marshalled by skilful discipline had fallen
To tributaries of all-conquering Rome.
Saw when Rome's grip, through fierce luxurious guilt,
Could hold no longer; and with tattered plume
Her eagles left her slaves to stem or tide
The hungry Pict incursions as they could.

Next when a burly genial race here raised
The White Horse Standard: men who wrought the soil
Till yellow corn, responsive, sunned the plains.
When, lured by booty, Ravens from the North
Bent hitherward: stiffly the contest tugged
Long years; till both the wearied champions joined
Their hands, as common home to share the Isle.
With peace the land grew fat; and wholesome bonds
Of nobles to their kings, and serfs to them,
Fell slackened or distorted to misrule;
When Norman William, hard as rocks and fierce
As fire, with charge of mailed horse and showers
Of steel, won England. Her rough sons he drilled
Grimly: by stern command and strength of sword
He forced obedience where he fixed a law.
For ages long against men's stubborn minds,
With give and take, the bold Plantagenets
Kept up the drill. At length the race, now grown
By constant wrestle into thews of power,
Moved calm with strength beneath the Tudor's sway.
And then a Northern Stuart wore their crown,
Whose son, unmindful he was over men
Truth-lovers, lied to them and lost his head;
For Puritans held no respect for lies.
Next flared Charles Satyr's saturnalia
Of Lely Nymphs, who panting sang "More gold;
We yield our beauties freely; gold, more gold."
Hapless explosions, folly, frenzied plots;
Till well coerced by Lowland William's craft.
Then plans that led to nought, or worse, enforced
By Marlborough's cannon thundering over-seas.
Then through the Guelphic line; our race now grows
To that great power which is to sway the world.

Down from those human shambles, wolf-belapt,
To when, in pardonably grand excess
Of pity, through our people's will was bought
Free indolence for Isles of Western slaves:
And now, when thousands blandly would deny
The proven murderer his rope, the thief
Due chastisement; and when a General
May blunder troops to death, yea, and receive
His Senate's vote of thanks and all made smooth;
And when, as much from universal trust
In other states' goodwill as from the pinch
Of blinking parsimony, we our fleets
Let rot, and regiments shrink to skeletons.—
From those fell rights to such urbanity

The march indeed is long; tho' kindly freaks
May sometimes clamour Justice from her throne;
Yet gentleness is still a noble gain,
And we will trust such freaks are nobly meant.

To touch the power we hold, what work has been
Of vigorous brawn, and keen contriving brains!
Stout men with mighty battle in their limbs;
Thinkers, whose cunning struck beyond the strength
Of hosts; priests sworn to God, whose daily lives
Preached gospel purity and kindliness;
Wise chroniclers, whose patience garnered facts
For present want and food for coming time;
And dames who made their homes a paradise,
And kept their husbands great;—have greatly given
The light and choicest substance of their lives
For generations mingling each with each,
Wave multitudinously urging wave,
Toward the one great broadening flow of things,
Then passed into the gloom that swallows all.

Could I dwell here in our proud Island Home,
Preserved by countless victories; made strong
By kings and kingly councillors; enriched
By artisans, whose skill surpassed all men's;
And by such wondrous song immortalised
It glorifies mankind: could I dwell here;
Here feed on this accumulated wealth,
Like senseless swine on acorns of the wood,
And own no wish to render thanks in kind?
Surely there could be found some waste wild flower
To yield one honey-drop that I might drain
To swell the general hive!

         At last resolved
Out to its utmost spray my force should strive,
And bring to fruit its yet unopened buds,
I, craving gracious aid of Heaven, straightway
Began the work which shall be mine till death.
If it be granted me that I disroot
Some evil weeds; or plant a seed, which time
Shall nourish to a tree of pleasant shade,
To wearied limbs a boon, and fair to view;
I then shall know the Hand that struck me down
Has been my guide into the paths of truth.

And She, my lost adored One, where is She?
Where has She been throughout these dragging years

Of labour?

She has been my light of life!
The lustrous dawn and radiance of the day
At noon: and She has burned the colours in
To richer depth across the sun at setting:
And my tired lids She closes: then, in dreams,
Descends a shaft of glory barred with stairs
And leads my spirit up where I behold
My dear ones lost. And thus through sleep, not death,
Remote from earthly cares and vexing jars,
I taste the stillness of the life to come.

What time his scythe in misty summer morns
With cheery ring the mower whets; and kine
Move slowly, breathing sweetness, toward the pail
Their milking-maid is jingling, as she calls
"Hi Strawberry and Blossom, hither Cows;"
While slung against the upland with his team
The ploughman dimly like a phantom glides:
What time that noisy spot of life, the lark,
Climbs, shrill with ecstasy, the trembling air;
And "Cuckoo, Cuckoo," baffling whence it comes,
Shouts the blithe egotist who cries himself;
And every hedge and coppice sings: What time
The lover, restless, through his waking dream,
Nigh wins the hoped-for great unknown delight,
Which never comes to flower, maybe; elsewhere,
The worshipped Maid, a folded rose o'er-rosed
By rosy dawn, asleep lies breathing smiles:
Then ofttime through the emptied London streets,
When every house is closed and spectral still,
And, save the sparrow chirping from the tower
Where tolls the passing time, all sounds are hushed;
Then walk I pondering on the ways of fate,
And file the past before me in review,
Counting my losses and my treasured gains,
And feel I lost a glory such as man
Can never know but once: but how there sprung
From out the chastening wear of grief, a scope
Of sobered interest bent on vaster ends
Than hitherto were mine; and sympathy
For struggling souls, that each held dear within
A sacred meaning, known or unrevealed:—
And these, in their complexities and far
Relations with the sum of general power
Which is the living world, now are my gain;
And grant my spirit from this widened truth

A glimpse of that high duty claimed of all.

How wildly flares the West about the sun,
Now fallen low! And as one, nameless, sails,
Lost deep in witching reverie, along
A silent river; passing villages
Busy with toil; flowered banks and shadowy coves,
And cattle browsing peaceful in the meads;
Who only wakes to consciousness, when full
A burst of sunshine from the sinking orb
Smiting the flood first strikes his dazzled sight;—
So to the present hour am I recalled
By yon red sun-light flaming up the spire,
And vane that sparkles in the warm blue heaven
And that too-well-remembered tolling bell.

Now on the broad mysterious ocean leans
The sailor o'er his vessel's side, and feels
The buzzing joys of home; wondering if fate
Will bear him on to end his being there.
Now pleased the housewife down the path descries
Her husband's footsteps hitherward; his meal
Prepared, the children each made tidy; she
With smiling comfort means to soothe her man,
By labour wearied, through the evening hours.
They whirl their life web, humming like a wheel,
These airy insects. Birds have ceased to sing,
But twitter faintly, settling to their rest;
And not a rook's caw rends the placid air.
I must begone; but ere I go, will kneel
To kiss this ivy—modest earthly type,
That would with constant verdure grace her name,
As I enshroud her memory with my love!
For She has been the blessing that has nerved
My strength in failing hours of blackest night,
When doubts oppress and fears distract; and when
Gigantic Evil's hoofs are crushing good,
And pity burns in terror; while, appalled,
Blanched Justice shrinks aloof; and not a voice,
The smallest, dares uplift itself against
The dripping blood-red horror which pollutes
With death and danger, heaven and earth and sea;
When men's belief grows wild, seeing alone
The dreadful black abominable sin,
Forgetful that the light still shines beyond;
And doubting last the very truth of God,
They hate their fellow creatures and themselves;
Groaning beneath a Despot, who thinks less

Of precious human blood, than shipwrights count
Of water in the dock, so many feet
Will bear so many tons, if it but aid
One little step his brutalising aims,
Who as an armed thief sacks his people's wealth.
Then shines my Love's star-brightness thro' the gloom;
And comes, as comes a glorious Conqueror
Returning from that Despot's overthrow,
His brow yet flashed and pale with victory:
Whose prowess long withstood the charging shocks
Of hosts that swarmed; who, baffling with his skill
Their cunning combinations, in good time
Closed his own force and wrought them utmost woe;
Smashed the huge liners of the hostile fleet,
Their swiftest frigates sank to watery hell:
Others he scared like fowls; and trailed the rest
In foamed victorious wake, a captured prize,
Where thronged his people stand in proud acclaim
Of "Welcome, Welcome, Welcome! To our hearts
O Saviour of thy country! to our hearts
O Father of thy people! welcome back!"
And shout in exultation his dear name;
Who moves through storms of music, and beholds
Gay seas of faces tossed with happiness,
And lit through rapture into wondering awe.
And as that grateful multitude forgets
Whatever wrong he may have done, do I
My scathing sorrow, and embrace the good.

And when, in after years, that honoured One
Returns at last unto his native land,
From having wrought his last great victory,
A solemn corpse; in state his people close,
Solemnly to do honour to the dead,
And stand in silence, mid the mournful sway
Of martial music wailing he is gone
Who saved them from the shackles they abhorred;
And in all reverence, with tenderest hands,
And tearful eyes, and hearts that burn and throb,
They lower their consecrated Hero down,
Down sinking slowly to his lasting rest:
Whose glory rises to a settled star
Lighting the land he loved for evermore.
So comes my love to me: its glorious light
Yet hovers sacredly, and guides me on
To grander prospects, and more noble use
Of powers entrusted me. Henceforth my soul
Will never lack a spot whither to flee,

When crowding evils war to shake my faith
In righteousness: for thinking of Her life
Made up of gracious act and sweet regard,
Compassionately tender; and enshrined
In such a form, that oft to my fond eyes
She seemed divine, I scarcely can withhold
My wonder Heaven could spare Her to a world
So stained as ours. And now, whatever come
Of wrong and bitterness to break my strength;
Whatever darkness may be mine to know;
A ray has pierced me from the highest heaven—
I have believed in worth; and do believe.

II. WORK

Sweet is the moisture of the trellis-rose
Dripping in music down through glistening leaves;
And sweeter still its fragrance that we breathe
On throwing wide our lattice to the morn.
Sweet to see thrushes bright-eyed speckle-bosomed,
Search dew-grey lawns with keen inspective glance;
And rabbits nimbly nibble tender grasses,
Or pause when startled at each other's shade.
And when the orchard boughs bend low with fruit,
With joy we watch the mounded harvest wains
Glide amid singing hedgerows smoothly by.
'Tis fair to watch hung pale in milky azure
Mist slowly closing into wandering cloud
Driven by the clean and light elastic wind;
And through that lone harmonious sunshine hum
Of unseen life mark how the floating seeds
Pass like flown fancies out beyond regard.

But sweeter than all roses, sights of birds,
Richer than fruit, more than whole lands of corn,
Fairer than glories of the brightest day,
Dearer than any old familiar sound
Of childhood hours, than every glittering joy
Thrown from the teeming fountain of the earth,
Is our impulsive answer to the call
Of Duty.

    They who would be something more
Than they who feast, and laugh and die, will hear
The voice of Duty, as the note of war,
Nerving their spirits to great enterprise,

And knitting every sinew for the charge.
It makes them quit a happy silvan life
For contest in the roaring capital.
And in its ever-widening roar stand firm
And fixed amid the thunder, foot to foot
With opposition, smiting for the truth.
To such the rage of battle charms beyond
The heaviest ocean-plunges dashed on cliffs,
The tempest's fury on the grinding woods,
Or elemental crashing in the heavens:
Beyond a lover's gladness when he feels
His maiden's bosom throbbing tremulously,
Beyond a father's when he feels in hand
The rounded warmth of little firstborn's limb,
Or in beholding him grown tall and strong:
And their delight will never wane, but wax
In greatness with the roll of time, and burn
More brightly fed with noble deeds. For souls
Obedient to divine impulse, who urge
Their force in steadfastness until the rocks
Be hewn of their obstruction, till the swamp's
Insatiability be choked and bound
A hardened road for traffic and disport,
Tall giant arches stride across the flood,
Till tortured earth release its mysteries
Which straight become slaves pliant unto man,
Till labours at the desk at length result
In law: who pondering on the stars proclaim
Their size and distance and pursue their course;
Who work whatever will give greater power
Or profit man with leisure to observe
The wondrous heavens and loveliness of earth;
Who will instruct him in the truth whereby
He learns to reverence more his fellow man;
Who point his spirit to the worshipping
Imperishable things, from which he comes
To scorn the fluttering vanities of wealth
As poisoned sweets and baubles should they dim
His eyes one instant to that awful light
Wherein he moves; who do and who have done
All that has ever aided man to free
Himself, imperfectly, from grosser self
And made his seeing pure:—such souls sublime
Will never want for blessed joy in work,
Working for Duty which can never die.

Men may seem playthings of ironic fate:
One stoutly shod paces a velvet sward;

And one is forced with naked feet to climb
Sharp slaty ways alive with scorpions,
While wolfish hunger strains to catch his throat;
One lingers o'er his purple draught and laughs,
One shuddering tastes his bitter cup and groans;
But there is hope for all. Though not for all
To sail through sunny ripples to the end,
Chatting of shipwrecks as pathetic tales;
All are not born to nurse the dainty pangs
That herald love's completion, and behold
Their darlings flourish in the tempered air
Of comfort till themselves become the springs
Of a yet milder race: all are not born
To touch majestic eminence and shine
Directing spirits in their nations' sight
And radiate unformed posterity:
But through transcendent mercy all are born
To enter on a nobler heritage
Than these, if each but wills to choose aright
In serving Duty, man's prerogative:
Which is far pleasanter than paths of flowers,
Than warmest clustering of household joys,
And prouder than the proudest shouts of fame
That follow action not in conscience wrought.

Fair Duty, most unlike the blight of death,
Whose dismal presence levels men to ruin,
Lifts up his nature into rarer life.
Hers is a broad estate open to poor
And rich alike: here rudest peasant may
Move as their equal with baronial lords,
And those who serve be great as those who rule:
Here a smirched artisan who merely bolts
The plates of iron fortress, breathes the pride
Of that trained chieftain who commands its guns;
And one that points or fires a single piece
Claims honour with the mind who planned the war.

Fair Duty, hard and perilous to serve,
Exacts devotion that is absolute,
Ere she reveal the heaven of her smile;
And gnaws with misery the traitor slave
Who having known her countenance and moved
At her behest relapses into sloth,
Or drudges serf to his own base desires:—
Sworn knight, and armed with mail and sword of proof,
But coaxing brutish ignorance with praise,
And with the wasted hearts of honest men

Gorging the monster he went forth to slay.
But whoso faithfully reveres her law
As primal, and of every want supreme,
Making edged danger discipline his strength,
That changes hindrance into past delight,
Fair Duty dowers with her celestial love,
From which the mystic blessing glory grows:
And glory born of Duty is a crown
Of light.

    And all thus crowned illume their work
In splendour that no earthly eye may pierce,
And know that every seed they set, and stone
They fix, and truth they reach, unite to found
A well-planned city in a governed land
That rising babes high a Temple built
Firm in its centre to the praise of God.
And each beholds his labours glorified,
Alike the toiler at the desk, a king
Upon his throne, or builder of the bridge:
The desk in lustre shines a kingly throne,
The throne diffuses radiance like a sun,
The bridge spans death—a pathway to the stars.

MARCH, 1865.

NELLY DALE

Ah, Nelly Dale, nigh fifty years
Since you and I set out together,
Joyful both, as the summer weather,
That swarmed our pathway to the meres
So rich with blossom, and opulent
Successive honeysuckle scent,
It smiled a golden garden, gay
With flutter of insects all the way!

The kine were white and smooth as silk
At Flowerdew's, where we went for milk
With jug and can. The can you bore
Jingled and tumbled when you tore
Your new frock striped with lilac, while
Crossing that high-built awkward stile.

Leaving our cottage gates at noon,
Adown the dusty hill we soon

Turned in a water-alley, dry
As our discourse; for we were shy,
Speaking not till the double ranks
Of willows on their shadowed banks
Had closed us from the road, and we
Were all we saw and cared to see.

As if let out from school we ran,
Until we settled stride for stride
To even walking, side by side;
And tho' to keep apart we tried,
The jug kept clinking against the can!

Once pausing in an upper path
That hemmed great pasture ribbed with math,
We saw the prospect openly
Melt in remote transparent sky;
Some fancy kindled, and I began
To whistle "Tom the Piper's Son,"
Wondering whether, when grown a man,
I should remain to plod, or plan,
As others about had always done,
Or to some wondrous country stray,
Over the hills and far away!

But turning to your comely face,
The opened flower of native grace
That casts a charm on homely ways,
Your mother's boast, her constant praise;
Contented here, I hoped I might
Be never from my darling's sight.

Ah, me, our young delight to roam
Along that lane so far from home!
Laughter, and chatter of this or that;
Ripening strawberries, mice and cat;
The birthday near; the birthday treat,
With something extra good to eat,
And currant, cowslip, elder wine,
As real lords and ladies dine!

Equal delight our silence next;
Making-believe that you are vext,
When swooping round to kiss you I
Tumble your bonnet all awry,
And promptly you the strings untie
To set it duly straight again;
How smartly twinkle ribands twain

To bows, turned sidewise in disdain,
Till by your nimble fingers fixed
They settle amicably mixed!

Moments of mutual mute surprise
Made converse of our glancing eyes,
As we went onward, all things seeming
Strange, and rich, and fair, while dreaming
Transient glimpses of what alone
Is ever by great-winged angels known.

We knew not whether you or I
First saw the splendid butterfly
Trembling about us as we turned
To watch how blue and crimson burned
In flashes 'twixt those blushing wings!
Nelly, I see you watch the lark
That fluttering high, aspiring sings;
We both watch till our sight grows dark,
And wonder whither he is fled
In sapphire ether overhead.
Tho' vanished, still his rapture rings
And thrills our bosoms, marching slow
Our winding way; when brilliant, lo
From somewhere starting, re-appears
Our friendly butterfly, and nears
A spider-web, in holly spun
With rainbow hues that net the sun,
Making coy circles ere he alight
Entangled in the toil of death!
Forward I spring, without my breath,
To see the fiend, high-elbowed, whirl
Around those limbs and wings, and twirl
His thread to thwart the chance of flight.
Fate on a single instant hangs,
And ready the demon's eager fangs
To penetrate that sylphic breast!
Nipping the wing-tips gently I
Flirt him from danger suddenly;
Strike with my cap a rapid blow,
Dashing the enemy down below
Thro' grass crushed safely into dust.
There shivering on my stretched forefinger
A little while his terrors linger,
Doubting if yet his wings to trust,
Ere, with a bolder flap or two,
He flutters into airy blue.

Could any mortal boy resist,
When heavenward, in a rosy pout
Your lips you offered to be kissed;
Fresh as carnations breaking out
Of dewy sheaths, on summer dawns
Yet pale upon the misty lawns!

We pass from shadowy splendour soon
To face the blazoned afternoon,
Where wide around the basking sun
Lies on the meadow fast asleep.
Near random bushes, one by one,
Nestled around a pond, the sheep
Are scattered and doze in graceful shade;
And hazed cornfields beyond the glade,
Undulating and dazzling sight,
Seem quivering for predestined flight
To worlds of unrevealed delight.
In lustrous sheen, their stately looks
Sedate as parsons reading books,
Flock grey-billed, see-saw-gaited rooks
Strutting; or when they wings assume
Pluck the warm air with fingered plume,
Labouring, anxious if weight and size
Make flight most hazardous or wise!

Nelly we sauntered on and on
By hedgerows, brightly overhung
And sprinkled thick with snowy showers
Of woodbine stars; where bindweed flowers
Ample and moon-white nobly shone,
And over green abysses slung,
Mid honey-haunted sound of bees,
Swayed lightly to the scented breeze.

In passing starwort's silvery gems,
By maple's warm fawn-tinted stems,
Caprices that gnarled the oak and thorn,
A sudden scream of rageful scorn
Startles us from the hedgerow nigh;
Whence two disturbed fierce blackbirds fly
Uttering threats of vengeance dire!
While we, who lit this angry fire,
Are wondering such discordant throats
Can tune those soft melodious notes
The fondest lover's listening ear,
At even, turns entranced to hear!

But if I sang of every sight
That afternoon which gave delight,
Those treasures would my numbers throng
Beyond the compass of my song;
Therefore, Nelly, to be precise,
We bought the milk, and paid the price
Charged in that rural paradise.
The rolls of butter, the jars of cream,
Churn, and cleanly pans, now seem,
Thro' fifty years of vanished time,
The memories of a nursery rhyme;
Or story, like The "Babes in the Wood,"
Written for children to make them good.

Homeward we went in soberer mood;
Haply the weight we had to carry,
By stile and gate oft made us tarry
To change our hands, and ease the weight
By making both co-operate.
At length we knew the hour grew late,
Because we saw our shadows rise,
Mocking our motions, thrice our size;
And keeping faithful phantom pace,
Tempting us to an elfin race
For fairy treasure; all in play!
For which, whatever they might say,
We knew our lives would have to pay!

Both breaking into prattle showed
How pleased we trod the dusty road
Once more; and rested where the rill
Sings issuing, halfway up the hill;
Where maids and wives their pitchers bring
To fill, and gossip at the spring.

To gossip ourselves we durst not stop,
As we had yet to reach the top
Where, starting from before the moon,
Our church spire quickened, rose, and danced
Higher and higher as we advanced,
And on a sudden ceased, as soon
As we were on the level; then,
There your mother stood at the gate
Impatient we were out so late;
Inquiring how, and why, and when;
She thought we had been drowned, and lost,
And by some savage mad bull tossed;
So long had she been looking out!

Whatever had we been about?

Altho' we saw so much that day,
But little then had we to say,
And told her a bewildered tale
Of garment torn by splintered rail;
Of spiders, blackbirds, butterflies;
Of rooks so near that looked so wise!
Of ghostly shadows, some of the way,
That had been tempting us to play,
Tho' sure they must have known we should
Be making all the haste we could!
The gentle scolding given and past,
We bade each other good-night at last
When floating in the stillness by
Came sounds like "late," and "supper," and "bed;"
And brighter through a deepening sky
A million stars shone o'er my head,
And bats flew fast and silently.

When memory wings her way to you,
I nurse my faith to think it true
For one day, Nelly, you were mine!
Ah, Dearest, had that day divine
Made us two one for good and all!
The nursery words I now recall,
Of Tom the Piper's Son's one tune,
Mused over in that day of June,
Have proved the prelude to my fate!
We were not fashioned to translate
Each other's will as man and wife:
And tho' I was not broken-hearted,
As Burns when from his Mary parted,
And fled the fragrance of his life;
Yet are you near and dear to me!
For on the bridge below the hill
I see you smile as sweetly still;
And in your clear wide-opened eyes
The spacious wonder of the skies.
While every thoughtful dainty grace
Rests well contented in your face,
All fascinations of the rose,
Uniting in your presence close.
Indeed, from glowing hair to feet,
So lightly poised, shaped so complete
You seem a being 'twixt a flower,
The glory of a shining hour,
And one ordained to satisfy

The claims of immortality.

Your beauty, like a queen's or king's
Good word, gives price to common things:
That can your ruddy fingers hold
Hangs lovelier there than purest gold;
And, as the poor, grown rich by chance,
Run raptured in extravagance,
My fancy riots in the fields'
Increasing wealth its charter yields:
And at your lintel, by the bower
Of vine leaves screening noonday heat;
The grapes, that hang there small and sour,
Are soft in bloom and more than sweet!

Beholding kittens as they play,
Black, tortoise, white, or silver grey;
Or ducklings on the water glide,
Yellow and soft, and artless eyed:
Or neatly-shapen chicks astray,
Pecking incessantly on their way;
Each such a trim completed creature,
In perfect movement, hue, and feature:
A foolish sadness makes me sigh
They lack immutability.
But you, my Nelly, are ever young.
Fresh and happy you dwell among
The brightest flowers, and flourish where
Meadows are ever fresh and fair.
As you were then I see you now,
Standing beneath an apple bough;
Your face amid its blossoms, bright
With rosy laughter and delight,
You seem a blossom the partial sun
Has chosen to make a larger one.

What may your pilgrimage have been,
Since both of us lost our Eden days,
I never rashly tried to glean;
And know not if your childhood ways
Were trodden by your maiden feet
When, flushed and shy with hope and fear,
You went your loitering swain to meet
And listen to sounds you loved to hear!
But if sometimes your heart was fain
Along our honeysuckle lane
Again to roam, in gracious flight
Your memory would have found delight

In wandering there a child again!

And if a matron you became,
With a matron's worries and daily strife;
The pain and sorrow, the hurt and blame
Mixed with pleasure, of being a wife,
I know not. But of this am sure,
That if with daughters you were blessed,
They found your bright example lure,
Thro' ways by wisdom proven best,
And sympathetic, generous trust
To kindly conduct more than just.

If old experience yet holds true,
And by a generation's lapse
Your daughter's child resembles you,
Then by that happy law perhaps
Another Nelly may be seen
To grace some other village green;
As native there as morning dew;
Or larks aloft, when lost to view
They lift us thro' the trembling blue
To soar with them in ecstasy;
Or primroses, whose welcome faces
From sunny banks and shady places,
Tenderly glimmer in pallid gold
Caught as early morning broke,
When, dreaming daylight they awoke
Enamoured from the moistened mold.
And if a Nelly, tho' changed in name,
Her fair endowments will the same
Point every grace that charmed before
Thro' unrenowned ancestresses,
Then still there beams a joy that blesses
The traveller by your cottage door;
Who, pleased in after years to trace
Remembrance of your playful face,
May linger on your presence while
Before him still you turn to smile.

www.ingramcontent.com/pod-product-compliance
Lightning Source LLC
Chambersburg PA
CBHW060049050426
42448CB00011B/2367